GERMANY'S
PUBLIC
SCHOOLS

by Horst Dichanz
and John A. Zahorik

Phi Delta Kappa
International Studies in Education

We can only see in a picture what our experience permits us to see.

Edgar Dale

The Phi Delta Kappa International Studies in Education Series was established as a way to enlarge the common experience of education by publishing studies that bring to readers knowledge of heretofore unfamiliar theories, philosophies, and practices in the profession of education.

As the interdependence of nations becomes increasingly evident and necessary with the passage of time, so too must our understandings about education become shared property. In thus sharing, we come increasingly to comprehend one another across civilizations and cultures, for education is at the core of human endeavor. Through education we pass on to succeeding generations not merely the accumulated wisdom of our past but the vision and means to create the future.

Changing Traditions in Germany's Public Schools is the fourth monograph in this series.

Previous titles:
Elementary Teacher Education in Korea
Teacher Education in the People's Republic of China
Innovation in Russian Schools

INTERNATIONAL STUDIES
IN EDUCATION

CHANGING TRADITIONS IN GERMANY'S PUBLIC SCHOOLS

by Horst Dichanz
and John A. Zahorik

PHI DELTA KAPPA
EDUCATIONAL FOUNDATION
Bloomington, Indiana
U.S.A.

Cover design by
Peg Caudell

Library of Congress Catalog Card Number 97-76529
ISBN 0-87367-396-4
Copyright © 1998 by Horst Dichanz and John Zahorik
Phi Delta Kappa Educational Foundation
Bloomington, Indiana U.S.A.

TABLE OF CONTENTS

Chapter 1
The Cultural Setting   1
   Political Development   3
   Geographic Factors   6
   Economic Conditions   7
   Social Traditions   9

Chapter 2
Bases of German Education   13
   Churches, Guilds, and Cities   15
   New Humanism and *Bildung*   18
   Reform Pedagogy in the 20th Century   20

Chapter 3
Modern School Organization   27
   Primary Education   29
   Elementary Education   29
   Secondary Education   30
   School Reform in the Former East Germany   32
   Establishing the *Gesamtschule*   33
   Vocational School, or *Berufsschule*   35
   Conclusion   38

Chapter 4
Teaching and Learning in German Schools   39
   Curriculum   42
   Instruction and Evaluation   44
   At the Elementary Level   46
   At the Secondary Level   48
   Teacher Training   50

School Finance 52

School Reform 53

Chapter 5

Three Case Studies 55

Ludgeri Grundschule 57

Max Planck Gymnasium 62

Hasperg Gesamtschule 68

Chapter 6

The Future: Problems and Promise 73

Current Issues 76

Promise 79

References 85

About the Authors 87

CHAPTER ONE
THE CULTURAL SETTING

To understand German elementary and secondary schools, it is necessary, first, to understand the country of which those schools are a part. Thus we examine the political, geographic, economic, and social aspects of Germany in this first chapter in order to set the stage for the information that follows.

Political Development

Until the end of the 19th century, there were only a few periods in which Germans were united in one state. They, like citizens in many other European states, were part of the changing political conditions for hundreds of years. German nationhood was influenced by the Romans, who tried to conquer the area north of the Alps called "Germania"; by Charles the Great (1747-1814), who subdued large parts of Europe; by Napoleon (1769-1821), who ruled many states in Europe; and, of course, by Adolf Hitler (1889-1945), who punished Europe with his dictatorship. There was, and still is, no "splendid isolation" for Germany or other European countries, such as the United States experienced for a time.

During the Middle Ages Europe was divided into dozens of small territories that were governed by noblemen from powerful families, such as the Hohenzollern, the Burgunders, and the Hapsburgs. Many of today's territorial and political conditions can be traced to this period of "absolutism," when rulers had few if any limitations on their power. During this time Prussia became the most powerful German state. Frederick II (ruled 1740-86) established an efficient and effective state administration, which also

3

served as an example for the other German states. Prussia is responsible for establishing the first German public school system.

The present nation of Germany was founded in 1948 after the Nazi regime was defeated. Under the control and supervision of the Allied Powers, Germany created its second democratic republic, the Federal Republic of Germany (FRG). The first one, the Weimar Republic, which was founded in 1914, had collapsed when Hitler came to power in 1933.

After a new constitution, the *Grundgesetz*, was approved in 1949, the western part of Germany was organized into 10 states and Berlin to form the Federal Republic. The national government was seated in the city of Bonn, and each of the states developed a center of state government. Berlin had been the national capital during the earlier period of a united Germany, and so the half called West Berlin was administered under special laws and agreements by the Allied Powers. However, that arrangement ended in 1991, when Germany was reunited.

After the Second World War, East Germany, or the Deutsche Democratische Republik (DDR), had been governed by the communists as a centralized state with East Berlin as its capital. The states of East Germany were added to those in West Germany by reunification. And, by 1999, if the present plan holds firm, the formerly divided city of Berlin again will become Germany's capital.

Since 1948, the Federal Republic of Germany had been a democratic state, as is now true of the reunited Germany. The main political parties in the national parliament include the Christian Democratic Union (CDU)/Christian Social Union (CSU), the Social Democratic Party (SPD), the Free Democratic Party (FDP), the Greens, and the Party of Democratic Socialists (PDS). At this writing, the CDU/CSU coalition holds the greatest number of seats, followed closely by the SPD.

The German federal government consists of two chambers: the *Bundestag* and the *Bundesrat*. The Bundestag is the assembly of the elected members of the parliament who represent the German population. Following the election of 1996, six parties gained seats in the parliament representing the voters of united Ger-

4

many's 16 states. The 672 members of the Bundestag work in many commissions and task forces, and they basically control the government and pass most of the laws.

In the Bundesrat, the second chamber, representatives of the states meet to discuss problems and pass laws that affect the state governments and their politics and responsibilities. Many laws need the agreement of the Bundestag as well as the Bundesrat before they become effective.

The federal government is headed by individuals elected to two important offices: the *Bundespräsident* and the *Bundeskanzler*. The Bundespräsident (or president) is the titular head of the government. The Bundespräsident is elected by the *Bundesversammlung*, an assembly that consists of members of the Bundestag and the Bundesrat. But the Bundespräsident functions mostly as a representative, or ceremonial, figure. The president is expected to be a nonpartisan, moral leader of the country.

The Bundeskanzler, or chancellor, is elected by a majority of the Bundestag and supported by his or her party or a coalition of parties. The Bundeskanzler is the actual head of the government and the chief of all the ministries and federal administrators, rather like Britain's prime minister.

In addition to these positions, the president of the *Bundesverfassungsgericht* (Federal Supreme Court) is one of the leading figures of the government. The Supreme Court holds a powerful position in the conduct of government because it interprets issues that come into dispute (for example, abortion, religion in public schools).

The states — which vary in size from the large cities of Hamburg and Bremen, which are states in themselves, to the land areas of Bavaria, North Rhine-Westphalia, or Mecklenburg-Vorpommern — are independent entities. Each has its own parliament, a minister/president or a mayor as the leader of the state government, and its own finance, legal, police, and education systems. Of course, there are many links with the central government; but the responsibility of the federal government is limited, and the states watch carefully that the central government does not regulate

5

areas that it should not regulate. The functions and responsibilities of all of these institutions are outlined in the *Grundgesetz*.

After the communist government of the DDR collapsed in 1989 and the Wall was dismantled, the DDR became part of the Federal Republic of Germany in 1990. When the population of the former DDR voted to enter the Federal Republic, they accepted the *Grundgesetz* as the common constitution for all Germans. The basic regulations were laid down in the *Vereinigungsvertrag* (contract of unification), which was signed in 1990. In addition to this contract, there were many other documents that regulated other aspects of the unification, such as a contract for the first election, an agreement that redefined the relations between the two German states and the Allied Powers, a declaration concerning the rights of the Allied Powers, and contracts concerning the borders with Poland and other socialist states. Many regulations were necessary to unify two countries that over the four decades of separation had developed different ideologies, histories, politics, economies, and cultures.

Additional regulations addressed many other problems, such as health and retirement insurance, standardization of working conditions and contracts, wage scales, disposal of the property of the former DDR government, treatment of political criminals in the justice system, election of government officials, and, not least of all, public education.

Although many of its neighbors suffered from the tyrannies of the Nazi regime during World War II, Germany now is accepted as a trusted European partner. Its political and economic connections to other European states, the open borders inside Europe, and the free flow of workers and tourists among the European nations all have caused Germany to become not merely an integral part of an increasingly interconnected European community but a leading advocate in the current movement toward a "United States of Europe."

Geographic Factors

Although Germany is known worldwide as an industrial country, it has much natural beauty, such as pine forests, green fields, and snow-capped mountains in the south and rolling flatlands and sandy shores in the north. The Rhine River flows through scenic valleys with picturesque vineyards and medieval castles that attract many foreign tourists. The fall of the communist government in East Germany opened other romantic areas in the east and southeast, which for decades could not be visited because of the closed borders of the communist regime.

With reunification, Germany now is a country of 80 million people in an area of 143,000 square miles. The irregularly shaped nation is some 370 miles wide and 500 miles long. It is $\frac{1}{26}$ the size of the United States, but it has one-third the population. Germany is one of the most populous countries of the world, with an average of 227 persons per square kilometer, trailing slightly behind more populous Belgium, the Netherlands, and Bangladesh. (By contrast, population density in the United States is 26 persons per square kilometer.) Germany, which is located in the center of Europe, shares borders with nine neighbor states. Thus it is hardly surprising that it is affected by tensions in other European countries, as most of them also are affected by Germany's internal currents.

However, because of this central location, Germany also functions as a link between Western and Eastern European states and between northern and southern European states. After its experience in the first and second World Wars, Germany no longer desires to be a European superstate. But because of its location and size, it cannot avoid occupying a leading position.

Economic Conditions

Germany has a few remaining natural resources, such as coal, iron ore, and silver; but mining is not an important industry today. Coal was mined until the 1960s; but after cheaper coal from Britain, Korea, and South Africa began to be imported, many coal mines were closed. The same is true for steel production. Today Germany's main resource is the human spirit.

Germany has a high standard of industrial production and well-trained workers, but they exact a price; industrial production has become very expensive in Germany. As the mining of natural resources became unprofitable, German industry focused more on the production of high-quality products. Cars, machinery of all types, optical equipment, medical instruments, and communication devices are some of Germany's main products in a heavily export-dependent economy. Strong unions supervise the working conditions in the plants; they bargain for new wages and other working conditions, and they participate in political discussion and action. On the one hand, Germany has become an expensive place for production; but on the other hand, one can find many highly skilled workers who are willing to work. In fact, German companies have the lowest strike rate of all the Western industrial nations.

The skills and reliability of the workers, as well as the capital and creativity of entrepreneurs, were the primary resources on which the "wirtschaftswunder" — the reconstruction of Germany's economy after World War II — was founded. The postwar recovery brought an economic boom that also required Germany to recruit workers from other European countries. Starting in the 1960s, Italian, Spanish, Yugoslavian, Greek, and Turkish workers migrated to Germany and joined the labor market. Of the workers in Germany today, 12% still are foreigners; and of these workers, 50% are from Turkey.

The foreign workers have been both a blessing and a problem for Germany. There is a saying: "We asked for workers, but it was human beings who came." Germany expected the workers to return to their home countries after their work ended, but many of them wanted to stay in Germany. However, to become a naturalized German is not an easy process. One must give up foreign citizenship before one can obtain German citizenship. At present, many foreign workers remain in Germany with temporary visas, while a considerable number of others work illegally. Since the eastern border was opened, additional workers from the formerly socialist states have fled into Germany seeking economic opportunities and a better life in the "Golden West."

Germany and its neighbors in Western Europe are now exploring new roads to common economic prosperity by joining together in a variety of ventures, including several transnational European organizations, such as the Council of Europe, the West European Union, and the Common Market. One of the current Common Market efforts is a move toward the establishment of a new European currency, called ECU, by the year 1999.

Social Traditions

Germans are hard workers. They save money for the future, they like cultural events, they celebrate holidays, and, like Japanese and Americans, they enjoy traveling. There is hardly any place in the world where one would not meet them. But Germany recognizes that present conditions may change in the future. After a recession in the early 1990s, there has been widespread discussion about whether Germany can afford to support its unemployed and homeless, its pensions, and other aspects of its renowned social welfare system. Unemployment reached 12% in 1997.

Income taxes to pay for these benefits have reached a level of 48%, higher than in most other industrialized countries. That means, for most workers, that half the year is spent working just to pay taxes. As a July newspaper proclaimed: "Up to today you worked for the state and the insurance companies; from today you work for yourself." There is growing protest against such high taxes. And economists are discussing how — and whether — the social welfare system can continue. Political parties and lobbyists for industrial and union groups are urging a total restructuring.

For readers who are unfamiliar with the German social welfare system, also termed the "social security system," it is useful to understand that it is one of the most comprehensive in the world. Indeed, the term "welfare" is used quite differently in this context than in the American welfare system, which is designed to benefit only the poor. German social welfare comprises three elements: a health care system, a pension system, and an unemployment system.

Health care. Every German citizen has health insurance that covers the basic costs of medical care. According to a person's income, he or she is either a member of a compulsory health insurance plan, which is paid half by the member and half by the employer, or may choose among several competing insurance companies that offer various services. Only when a person's income is more than 6,000 DM per month (about $4,000 in 1996) is he or she wholly responsible for medical costs.

Also, since 1995, all Germans are required to have *Pfegeversicherung*, or care insurance, to pay the costs of permanent medical care for those who need it. The total costs for general health care and permanent medical care insurance take about 14% of a worker's income. (Individuals who are out of work receive financial support from a state agency as part of the social welfare system.) Many physicians collaborate with insurance companies and are the preferred physicians of these companies, but in general people can choose their own doctors.

Pensions. The pension system has a similar structure to the health care system. Up to an income of 8,000 DM per month (about $5,000 in 1996), every employee is required to pay about 19% of his or her income into a pension account. For the wealthy there is no such regulation; they have to take care of their own pension and usually do so by purchasing personal insurance that will be paid out when they retire.

Unemployment. To protect workers from the consequences of joblessness, each person also pays into a general state unemployment insurance scheme. When a person becomes jobless, the individual gets up to 65% of his or her most recent income. After two years, support drops to 55%. Only when these phases of protection end does the individual draw social welfare support in a manner similar to the U.S. system. Refugees from other countries who legally come to Germany also receive social welfare benefits, including basic health care.

The social welfare system also regulates other matters related to worker security and well-being. For example, new mothers are provided with a three-month period to take care of their babies. During this time they receive a basic payment from their health insurance and are protected from being fired. After those three months, they may receive an education leave for up to three years, during which time they can continue to receive some financial support.

Other protections against being fired also are incorporated into the system, and these protections usually increase for individuals according to their length of employment. On a large scale, when a business closes or fires workers, a workers' committee has to agree to the company's proposals about how the business will help the unemployed workers and protect those (and any remaining) individuals' interests. However, as might be imagined, when economic conditions are in a downturn, as they are at this writing, a shrinking labor market makes such protections very difficult to maintain.

Even the holidays that every worker has a right to take are part of this social system. For example, with the rising postwar economy, the number of holidays every worker may take also has grown. Fully paid vacations start at 10 days when a person begins a job and often can increases to 28 days for someone who has worked for more than 25 years.

The social welfare system has greatly contributed to the stability of German society and its economy. However, many in Germany believe that the system may be strained to the limit. Since the beginning of the 1990s, there has been concern about the overall costs of this system. Economists complain about the high cost of social services that, in turn, raise production costs and decrease German competitiveness in the world market. As a consequence, many companies have moved their plants into countries with lower costs for workers. And so the government has begun cutting into the social security system.

The tradition of support for the poor and the protection of workers is strong in Germany and can be traced back to the early craftsmen associations of the 19th century, the social responsibility of the big churches, and the social tradition of the Social Democratic Party and the unions. However, modern necessity likely will mean more cuts in this expensive protection system. Individuals will shoulder more of the burden, while the responsibility of the state will shrink.

CHAPTER TWO
BASES OF GERMAN EDUCATION

It is unnecessary to delve much further back into history than the 16th century to understand German education in the 20th century. However, this 400-year period is useful grounding, and so in this chapter we take up the important people and events from this period that have influenced the nature of present-day schools in Germany. Readers should keep in mind that the German schools, like those in most other countries, have developed in accordance with the prevailing influences of their times. Politics is never far from education.

Churches, Guilds, and Cities

The Christian church from its inception highly valued education. Up to the Reformation in the 16th century, the Christian church was the only institution that offered formal schooling. In schools called *Domschulen* (church schools), *Klosterschulen* (monastery schools), or *Latein Schulen* (Latin schools), young men, mainly from the nobility, were educated to become priests and to assume church or secular office. Some noblemen were schooled by servant tutors who lived with them. And some noblemen were trained, particularly in fighting and war strategy, in "Ritterakademien" (knights' academies). Women generally were not schooled, except for some women who lived in convents.

One of the most important and powerful church orders for men at that time was the "Societas Jesu," founded in 1534 in Paris and later called the Jesuits. This order understood and practiced the German saying, "Wissen ist Macht" (knowledge is power). Because church authorities realized the importance of education, they kept it under their control and limited the people who were allowed to be educated to the clergy and nobility. Even in the monasteries a hierarchy existed that limited the monks' access to books. Only experienced monks, supervised by reliable older monks, were allowed to read. It was believed that nobody should know "too much." Knowledge could potentially endanger the positions and the privileges of the clergy and the nobility.

During the Reformation and the Renaissance (16th and 17th centuries) the church's influence on education began to decline. Expanded world exploration, a growing number of scientific discoveries, and the invention of movable type for mass publication all combined to provoke a questioning of conventions — including the church's authority over education. Indeed, a popular idea arose that people should use their intellectual powers to free themselves from the constraints of religion. Later, the philosophies of John Locke, Baron Montesquieu, and David Hume were cornerstones for a new period, called the Enlightenment (18th century). They focused on the conviction that human beings would think for themselves and organize their lives without being supervised or guided by the church or a sovereign. A person's ideas, interests, or wishes should not be limited. Human beings began to be seen as independent and self-directed individuals.

As these philosophical ideas became more and more concrete over a period of three hundred years or so, the church's power of education waned. People began to believe that the church was not a creation of God but that it was built by some men to establish and to protect their power over other men. Thus a movement arose around the notion that an independent and self-conscious citizenry required education to free them from the church's influence. Schooling, it began to be evident, was a "commodity" to which all men — and eventually women — were entitled.

These philosophical (in some cases, frankly anti-church) sentiments were given greater strength by the state's recognition of the power of education to affect commerce and the wealth of the state. To develop trade abroad and to strengthen commerce at home, the state needed educated people with knowledge in science, engineering, and accounting. In this period of "mercantilism" the intention to extend state power and trade became a driving reason to require a basic education for all. City councils and major craft guilds became interested in public education and started their own education institutions as counterparts of the church schools. City councils, for example, founded city schools called *Stadt-schulen* and *Magistratsschulen*; and the guilds developed a system to train and educate young people in various crafts.

In 1642 the Prince of Gotha issued the first universal school order, "Gothaische Schulmethodus," which regulated school organization, curriculum, teaching methods, exams, text books, and disciplinary matters. But, more important, it established mandatory education for all children. The law required children to attend school from about age 6 until they were judged to be "ready for life." The state of Prussia followed in 1763 with its "General-Landschul-Reglement," in which compulsory school attendance, supervision of teachers by church inspectors, a curriculum for a general education, and the idea of teacher training in teachers colleges were established.

All of these developments led to today's German public education system: a state-financed, state-controlled, three-track public school system and vocational education system that includes a state curriculum taught in vocational schools and practical training carried out in businesses and industries. This multi-layered system has direct ties to the earlier schools:

- Lateinschulen, Domschulen, and Kosterschulen can be regarded as precursors to the Gymnasium, which led the children of the upper class to the university. Until the 1960s the Gymnasium was the only way to enter a university.
- *Mittelschulen* and *Realschulen* were founded in response to the needs of trades and craftspeople who lived in the big cities. Even today these middle schools attract students from middle-class families who want a nonacademic education that focuses on middle-level professions.
- The *Volksschule*, today called the *Hauptschule*, is the type of school that requires compulsory school attendance for every

child regardless of family background. It was introduced, expanded, and administered as a Stadtschule or Magistratsschule, which had to take care of the education of all children who did not enter one of the other types of schools. Either independent city councils or the sovereign of a state issue regulations to be executed by the local administrations, because independent school boards do not exist in Germany as they do in the United States.

New Humanism and *Bildung*

Until the 19th century the education that students actually received in all types of schools was pretty rigid and narrow. This situation changed, in part, because it was influenced by the writings of several well-known authors: Herder, a romantic poet and philosopher; Goethe, an important scholar, philosopher, administrator, and the author of numerous novels, dramas, and poems; and Schiller, who was known for his revolutionary dramas, poems, and philosophical thoughts about freedom as a human right. Along with other philosophers and historians, these writers brought about a period in education called "classic-idealistic," in which the idea of a general personal education was based on an education philosophy called *Neuhumanismus*, or New Humanism.

Neuhumanismus focused on a broad, general education by which the individual was to become intellectually well-rounded. Whereas the German Renaissance brought back to life many of the ideas from ancient Roman culture and philosophy, Neuhumanismus went further back, to the ideals and philosophy of Plato, Aristotle, and other Greeks. One of the main ideas to rise out of this philosophical archeology was the relationship between the individual and the social community that is the essence of *Bildung*. Although difficult to translate, Bildung is both a set of ideals and a methodology. Its focus is on the tension that exists between an individual and the society in which he or she resides. The individual must be prepared to function in the society, yet the social framework also must respect the sanctity of the individual.

Education, from the perspective of Bildung, strives to help students become self-determining, free, critical individuals but not without regard to social realities and the possibility of creating new social relationships.

One of the most important philosophers of Neuhumanismus was Wilhelm von Humboldt (1767-1835). During the single year that he served as head of the Department of Public Instruction of the state of Prussia, he developed an organizational plan for public education in Prussia that completely changed the existing structure. The education system that he proposed consisted of three levels, which still are evident in modern German schools:

- An elementary school for basic education in the mother tongue and in basic accounting.
- A Gymnasium that focused on a historically oriented, a science-based, or a foreign language-based curriculum. (Although students were asked to choose their individual focus, they had to study the basics in each of these fields. In this way, Humboldt tried to ensure that every student was educated to become a harmonious, well-rounded person familiar with a broad spectrum of real life. However, as a result of the former influence of the church, students were taught only in Latin.)
- A university for individuals interested in scholarship. The goal of the university was to guide young people to become questioning and searching individuals who explored the problems of science and who found philosophy to be the core of scholarly thinking.

The importance of the Neuhumanismus philosophy, particularly for the development of the Gymnasium and the university, can hardly be overestimated. Although educational tasks have changed — and thus the goals of education have been adapted since 1800 — the ideas of Humboldt are still the basis for German secondary and postsecondary education today.

While Humboldt and his successors focused on academic, general education for everyone, other groups and institutions had different ideas about education. As mercantilism continued to grow in the cities, so did interest in preparing educated persons for the business world. The guilds were interested in training workers for the various crafts and trades. They looked for an education that focused on the "real" things of life. Thus many guilds adopted the ideas and models developed by Hecker in Berlin, who started the first private "Realschule" in 1747. Hecker's schools stressed an economic-mathematic curriculum. Latin was not required. The idea was to prepare students to take positions in trade, administration, and banking; and so the goals of the Realschule were to produce students who were industrious, reliable, and trained in the "three R's" and other areas of basic knowledge. To earn a Realschule graduation certificate in 1832, one had to pass an exam in German, French, math, science, history, geography, and Latin or English.

As can be seen in this brief overview, during the 19th century two main trends developed in the German education system. One was that the administration of the schools changed from religious to secular. Churches lost control and influence in favor of state, municipal, and guild control of schools. This generally came to be regarded as a positive movement, a view that solidified after the unification of the German state in the 1870s.

However, the other trend was that differentiation of school organization became more pronounced and, viewed negatively, more rigid. The three different types of schools that were established early on — the Volksschule (later to become the Hauptschule), the Realschule, and the Gymnasium — became entrenched. In each of these types of schools, the curriculum became more and more fixed; and the teaching style of teachers grew less flexible as a consequence. Therefore, by the turn of the century, many educators and philosophers were calling for the reform of public schools.

Reform Pedagogy in the 20th Century

A vivid intellectual and spiritual atmosphere in Germany and Europe existed as the 20th century opened. Scientific thinking was growing, and people relied more on their own rational capacity. The status of the rich and powerful was being shaken by the social and democratic movements that spread from France to the rest of Europe.

Schools were observed more critically than ever before. During the previous century the teaching methods of Johann Friedrich Herbart (1776-1841) had begun to influence teacher training and teaching practices in Prussia and in other parts of Germany. Herbart had taken pedagogical ideas from the Swiss pedagogue, Johann Heinrich Pestalozzi (1746-1827), and added recommendations based on psychology to develop more structured teaching skills for teachers. But the skills often were employed mechanically and mindlessly and made learning in public schools an exercise that did not motivate students to learn. Students were forced to learn only what their teachers, the curriculum, and the school offered them. No one was interested in the question of what the students themselves wanted to learn or believed they needed to learn.

As a result of this stultifying environment, physicians, teachers, and philosophers from different countries of Europe developed new approaches and teaching practices, and a new period of reform pedagogy (*Reformpädagogik*) spread across the continent. The ideas of a number of these reform pedagogues, including the following individuals (not all of whom are German), came to influence modern German schools.

Maria Montessori. The first female Italian physician, Maria Montessori (1870-1952), was an extraordinary woman. She first worked with mentally retarded children in a Rome hospital. By carefully and patiently watching these children, who often came from poor families, she discovered that they were more able than she expected. Indeed, she found that they did not need to be supervised but, rather, needed to be encouraged to rely on themselves.

Both her medical experience and her deep conviction regarding the positive potential of every child caused her not only to develop new methods of treatment for mentally retarded children but also to fight for better teaching of all children. To give children from poor families a better chance, she founded "children's houses," preschools for young children, in those areas of Rome where many poor families lived. Her ideas received notice and recognition everywhere.

Montessori fundamentally believed that every child has a "plan of mind." Therefore, every child could grow into a mature human being on his or her own. The environment, including parents and teachers, was nothing but "material" for this individual plan of development that could function as stimulation and motivation. The execution was up to the child. By working with real objects, the child would be able to find his or her way from chaos to a clear classification, from his or her sense impression to the concept or meaning of things. Thus the central task of the teacher was to give children the opportunity to experience real things. Because of the limited experiences available to many children in cities and to make sure that every child got the chance for certain experiences, Montessori developed and used specially prepared learning materials.

These materials were — and still are — one of the elements of her practical pedagogy. For example, children had to fit differently shaped pieces of wood into holes, build orders of stones into a rising row, sort containers filled with materials to a particular order, and so on. The learning materials function as a "materialized" curriculum, which teachers and students must carefully follow.

Montessori schools in Germany today are usually private schools; but if they are state certified, then they are publicly supported for up to 90% of their costs. Many elementary Montessori schools exist in Germany; and as a consequence of the criticism of public schools, the demand for more Montessori schools is growing. Montessori schools are regarded as alternative schools that provide a specific kind of education, but the basic philosophy has influenced regular German schools, particularly at the elementary level.

Peter Petersen. Another popular type of alternative school is the *Jena-Plan-Schule*, or *Peter-Petersen-Schule*. This school is based on the pedagogical ideas of Peter Petersen (1884-1952), a teacher, principal, and professor of education, who worked at Hamburg, Halle, and Jena. Petersen criticized public schools for dividing lessons into 45-minute segments and content into separate subjects. He also regarded the separation of students by age as unnatural. In Petersen's schools, particularly in an experimental school at the University of Jena, he used another approach. His idea was to offer students a learning environment that motivated them to learn and to feel good about themselves. He wanted the school to be a place of *Lebensgemeinschaft* (vivid community) and the classroom to be a *Wohnstube* (living room). He put the students together in age groups of three years and organized three different learning groups that he called *Stammgruppen*. When students were promoted to the next grade, they stayed in their Stammgruppe for two more years. This procedure allowed the students to build close relationships with their classmates, and it gave the teacher a chance to really know the students.

The practical ideas of Petersen became quite popular. His influence today is based mainly on his book, *Der Kleine Jena-Plan* (1927), in which he explains his practical pedagogical ideas about how to organize teaching based on students' real lives, instead of on books. However, his philosophy and understanding of society, its classes and orders, is questionable; and his notions of democracy have become unacceptable. Because of his unusual philosophical ideas and his political behavior during the Nazi regime, Petersen often is criticized nowadays. But his recommendations for teaching are supported and have been adopted into practice.

Today there are only 40 Jena-Plan-Schulen in Germany, but Petersen's ideas of multi-year grouping of students, making the school a family-like home, and focusing on the needs of students have been widely adopted by schools in Germany and elsewhere.

Rudolf Steiner. Another important German pedagogue was Rudolf Steiner, the founder of the Waldorf Pedagogy and Waldorf Schools. Rudolf Steiner (1861-1925) developed a philosophy that he called "anthroposophy," a philosophy that distinguished several stages of world development. Steiner believed that every human being has to repeat these stages in his or her personal development. Steiner believed that growth is organized in three stages, or phases, of seven years each. After Steiner published his ideas on education, he was able to convince the owner of a large cigarette-manufacturing company, Waldorf-Astoria, of the usefulness of such an education for the children of its workers. Together company officials and Steiner agreed to establish a school based on these ideas in Stuttgart in 1919 for the Waldorf workers' children.

Since that time, Waldorf Schools have become popular because they support the development of each child's individuality; they strengthen understanding in the arts; and they view music, dancing, gymnastics, and the fine arts as expressions of the individuality of a person.

Today there are 157 Waldorf Schools in Germany as private schools. However, some of the Waldorf Schools that meet the requirements of public schools also receive financial support from the states. To become a Waldorf-School teacher, one needs, in addition to the state-required university training, training in a Waldorf teacher training college, much as Montessori teachers receive special training in Maria Montessori's methods. Waldorf Schools also have been founded in many other countries, including the United States, and now number about 630 worldwide. As in the other cases, the ideas put forward by Steiner also have influenced German public schools generally.

Hermann Lietz. Another German pedagogue of the beginning of this century was Hermann Lietz (1868-1919). His main interest was to protect children from the growing dangers of modern civilization, particularly in the urban areas. He founded several schools that he placed in rural settings by purchasing country houses or farms and transforming them into *Landerziehungsheime* (rural boarding schools). To make the environment wholly educative, he enlarged the responsibility of the teachers by placing the students together with the teachers' families. They formed education groups that included the teacher's wife, the teacher's own children, and seven to 10 students who all lived together.

Lietz wanted to ensure a lifelong learning attitude on the part of the students. Thus his schools emphasized practical training as well as academic learning and permitted students to participate in making decisions about school matters. He also paid attention to a healthy life, offered sports and outdoor activities, and prohibited the use of drugs.

Lietz's schools were attractive to parents who worked full time and did not have time to educate their children. Lietz also accepted students with behavior problems, because they could be supervised and educated day and night at his schools.

The Landerziehungsheime movement led to the creation of more than 50 such boarding schools across Germany, such as the Schloss Salem near Meersburg and the Odenwald Schule in the Schwarzwald. And similar Landerziehungsheime, such as the school in LaPorte, Indiana, were developed in the United States. Lietz-type schools, which normally are privately funded by high tuition, still attract students. Their pedagogical work, which is well-regarded, has had some effect on the German Grundschule.

Georg Kerschensteiner. Georg Kerschensteiner (1854-1932) had quite a different pedagogical philosophy. When he worked as a city superintendent at Munich, he saw the problems of young people who could not find employment after they had finished the Volksschule at age 14. After years of struggle, he started a school in Munich that was the forerunner of the modern vocational school. It was designed as a part-time school that students could attend for several hours each week while they worked at their jobs.

In addition to academic studies, the students worked in businesses, offices, and factories to learn practical skills. From this simple beginning grew the educational structure that now is known as the German "dual system" and is, in part, responsible for the quality of German workers and the high value placed on German products.

Celestine Freinet. The French pedagogue Celestine Freinet (1896-1966) was known for his focus on teaching through active learning, instead of teaching with textbooks. He did not trust traditional means of teaching and experimented with various methods of facilitating students' learning. He advocated working with printing sets, rather than writing by hand. And because children were released from the burden of handwriting, they were able to focus more on composing.

This method of using printed letters to express oneself became widely known in Europe and is used in many German schools as a means to motivate students to develop their written composition skills and to strengthen their self-confidence.

From this brief catalogue of major figures, one can readily see that the current practices and procedures in German schools have evolved from many sources. The dual focus on both academic and vocational education always has been central, but also important has been — and is — careful attention to the individual as a self-governing person with a strong social conscience.

CHAPTER THREE

MODERN SCHOOL ORGANIZATION

The legal status of education in Germany is similar to that in the United States. The central government has no responsibility for elementary and secondary education but only, and then partially, for higher education and vocational education. In the *Grundgesetz* of 1949 only a single paragraph deals with education. It states that the school system is controlled by the states and that the care and education of the children are the natural right and obligation of parents.

Thus all of the basic aspects of education are regulated by the 16 states, which are autonomous in terms of cultural and educational issues. As a consequence, one will find 16 different school systems in terms of aims and organization.

Primary Education

Primary education — preschool and kindergarten, in U.S. terms — is voluntary. Many of these institutions are run by churches or other private agencies. Since 1996 every child has had the right to attend a state-supported kindergarten. About 80% of parents send their children to a daycare center or a kindergarten. Some parents also send their children to a *Vorschule* (preschool) that provides services for at-risk children.

Elementary Education

The elementary school, or *Grundschule* (first through fourth grade), is the only comprehensive school that all children *must* attend. After they leave the elementary school, the students are divided among several types of secondary schools.

Secondary Education

Students (and their parents) theoretically can choose from among four types of secondary schools: *Hauptschule, Realschule, Gesamtschule,* and *Gymnasium*. As school choice usually determines one's future career, this choice of secondary school is extremely important. The student population, as of the mid-1990s, was divided among these schools in roughly the following proportions: Hauptschule, 25%; Realschule, 34%; Gesamtschule, 13%; and Gymnasium, 28%.

However, this distribution is not entirely consistent with parents' wishes. According to Rolff and his colleagues (1990), 12% of the parents prefer the Hauptschule for their children, 36% prefer the Realschule, and 52% prefer the Gymnasium. (Preference for the Gesamtschule was not ascertained.)

When children leave the elementary school, their teachers write a report about their performance and give a recommendation to the parents concerning which type of school they think best suits the student. In some states the schools also incorporate an *Orientierungsstufe,* or orientation phase, that is intended to help students and teachers to determine the type of a secondary school the students should attend.

Hauptschule. The Hauptschule was founded in the 1960s as a successor to the *Volksschule,* a normal school for lower-achieving poor children. The Hauptschule includes grades 5 through 10 and offers a curriculum oriented toward the labor market. Students are taught the basics, but they also are taught practical skills and have work-related experiences out of school through field trips and on-the-job training. Many of the students who graduate from the Hauptschule will be directly employed in businesses. Others may continue their education in technical colleges after they have successfully finished an apprenticeship.

Realschule. The Realschule was founded at the beginning of the 19th century by city magistrates and business people as a reaction to the growing importance of the Gymnasium, which prepared only students interested in a university (academic) education. The city administrations and businesses needed people with basic skills and knowledge in German, science, and mathematics and who had no particular interest in academe.

The turn-of-the-century Realschule offered a curriculum that focused on the realities of life in the big city and how to function effectively in that environment. These middle-class schools were founded by middle-class citizens and emphasized their values and lifestyles. The Realschule still maintains this character today. There have been few reforms in the Realschule, and it has not been significantly influenced by changes in the political landscape.

Gymnasium. The Gymnasium is the oldest and most highly regarded type of school in Germany. Its origin can be traced back to the old Latin and church schools of the late Middle Ages and the Neuhumanismus of Humboldt. Although he was in office for only one year, Humboldt's ideas were important for the development of the Gymnasium. In particular, the idea of a *gebildete* person (a well-rounded, well-educated, mature person) became the goal of the education philosophy of the Gymnasium — a goal that has never changed, in spite of many changes in curriculum and structure over time.

Humboldt stated that the aim of the Gymnasium was to give students a broad education that would serve as a foundation for the university. In comparison to this broad general education, he believed that specific professional education was of minor value. This philosophical orientation has permeated all levels of education and contributes even today to the belief that such general education and theoretical training are of greater value than practical, vocational education.

Until the 1970s the Gymnasium was mainly the university preparation school for upper-class children who were destined to assume positions in administration, politics, education, culture, and business. However, since that time the minority of Gymnasium students from the working class has been growing.

From its origin, the Gymnasium has been the school that prepares students for the university. Students needed knowledge from 14 subjects. They needed to be able to analyze, construct, create, and formulate. Although this claim is still in effect, a change in the population of the Gymnasium has brought about a change in teaching and learning. The population of students in the Gymnasium has increased from 10% to 50% in some states. This has caused a move away from a teacher-centered, subject-only teaching approach. The Gymnasium had to adapt to the needs and abilities of its changing clientele.

Gesamtschule. When the Social Democratic Party under the leadership of Chancellor Willy Brandt came into office in 1969, many social reforms were initiated. One of the consequences of the reforms was the discussion of the values of a democratic society and the conditions of life in the future. As a result of these issues being raised, a number of states started to restructure their school systems. Some wanted to make it possible for students to transfer from one type of secondary school to another, based on the individual student's achievement. Others wanted to demolish the existing system of three secondary schools and replace it with one comprehensive school, or Gesamtschule, to be attended by all students.

In 1969 the Gesamtschule received public support when an independent national education board, the *Deutscher Bildungsrat*, recommended the establishment of 30 Gesamtschulen on an experimental basis. In a political battle that lasted for the next 20 years, those in favor of the Gesamtschule have been successful. The Gesamtschule is now a regular part of the public school system in 10 of the 16 states. In no state, however, was the traditional three-track system replaced by the Gesamtschule. In some states the Gesamtschule has become a new, fourth track in the regular system; in others it still is viewed as an experiment.

School Reform in the Former East Germany

A few words must be said about the schools of the former East Germany. After the Wall came down, the reorganization and reform of East German schools to bring them up to the standard of their West German counterparts was a daunting challenge. The East German schools had been centrally controlled by the government in East Berlin and now had to be completely restructured.

Most of the former school administrators left office or were thrown out of office by the parents, new democratic groups, or politicians from the West. Thus for several years the situation in public education, as in many other areas, was chaotic. New state parliaments needed to be elected, and new laws regarding the public schools needed to be established.

Today the basic reorganization has been largely completed, though many details still demand attention, from expanding teacher education to upgrading school facilities. The five "new" states have created new systems of public education, most of them quite similar in organization to those in the West.

However, none of the former East German states established Gesamtschulen, because they wanted to avoid the political divisiveness over this type of school form. Some of the states also avoided using the Hauptschule because of its poor reputation and, instead, created the *Mittelschule*, which is a combination of the Hauptschule and the Realschule. Other special considerations also were taken up in the Eastern states. For example, Brandenburg established the new subject of ethics because it did not want to teach religion from a particular orientation, such as Catholicism and Protestantism.

The reorganization of the public schools in the East according to democratic ideas was heavily supported by the Western states. They sent personnel to the new states to help them develop their education systems. But now the Eastern states no longer seek guidance from the "Wessi's" (experts from the West) who, admittedly, served Eastern interests but also served the particular interests of the West.

Establishing the *Gesamtschule*

As Germany's newest school form, the Gesamtschule deserves a fuller explanation. The goals of the Gesamtschule were based on ideas from comprehensive systems in Sweden, Great Britain, and the United States. These goals were: 1) to equalize opportunity for all children, particularly children from low-income families; 2) to change the school from a bureaucratic system to a democratic one; 3) to enhance the social learning of children; and 4) to add communication skills to the curriculum.

Many educators and psychologists argued that it is not legitimate to assess students at the end of the fourth grade according to their achievements and abilities and then to assign them to the different types of schools on that basis. With the creation of the Gesamtschule, the division of students into the traditional three-track system could be avoided.

Of course, the Gesamtschule had to function under the same laws as the other schools. But because it was new, it was watched more closely. The public had high expectations and wanted to control these schools, and so the Gesamtschule had to endure many research projects. But, as a result, there is no other type of school about which we have lately learned so much.

Some of the most important results of the evaluation of the Gesamtschule are as follows (Fend 1982):

- The Gesamtschule has attracted many students from low-income families, and a higher proportion of students have been able to transfer to the Gymnasium than occurred under the former three-track-system.
- The Gesamtschule has developed a positive school climate; students like school and are motivated through interest, rather than through fear of failure. The Gesamtschule has facilitated social learning through appropriate school settings better than the other models have done.
- The Gesamtschule has developed new forms of school and staff organization, and school buildings have been opened to the community.
- The Gesamtschule has experimented successfully with new forms of teaching based on students' needs and interests; teachers emphasize learning how to learn, instead of simply acquiring isolated content.

Although these results are very positive, the Gesamtschule has not yet been accepted by the public in general. Comparatively few parents send their children to the Gesamtschule. And, in fact, in some states there is much more demand for Gesamtschulen than in others. This demand ranges from only two Gesamtschulen (as of 1989-90) in Bayern (Bavaria) to 131 in Nordrhein-Westfalen (North Rhine-Westphalia). And it should be remembered, too, that none exist in the five Eastern states.

When the Gesamtschule was evaluated at the end of the 1980s, it was found that the equality of opportunity of children from all classes had risen. But such an evaluation has not been universal. The 1990 *Jahrbuch* noted, "There is no decrease in the inequality of education opportunity between different social classes. . . . The opportunity to receive a higher education at a Gymnasium or a university has become more unequal" (Rolff et al. 1990, p. 60).

By the middle of the 1990s a group of Gesamtschule teachers had started a campaign to expose the growing difficulties and poor conditions that existed in the Gesamtschule. Where this campaign will end is unclear, but it is obvious that the political status of the Gesamtschule, as a type of reform school, has been weakened. Although education experts support the Gesamtschule as an innovative, effective reform — some schools received awards for pedagogical excellence from the Carl Bertelsmann Foundation in 1996 — the majority of the parents and teachers prefer not to change the school system as a whole.

The Gesamtschule as an entity might be in danger, but its concept of a new learning approach has had a significant effect on the public school system as a whole. Most of the teaching innovations of the last 20 years are a result of the experimentation done in the Gesamtschule. More and more schools of all types are retraining their teachers to be able to work with students in an approach that stresses understanding and independent thinking.

Vocational School, or *Berufsschule*

Whereas the different tracks take care of general education for the students, the *Berufsschule*, or public vocational school, is responsible for vocational education. The Berufsschule is framed and structured by the states and organized by the cities, communities, or counties. It is widely differentiated and provides continuing education in the basics and in various occupations.

Education for the 49% of the student population that enrolls in a vocational school takes place partly in the school itself and partly in the workplace, where students are taught skills necessary in their particular field. Businesses spend a lot of energy and money training apprentices, because they want productive workers in the future.

The *Berufsausbildung* (vocational curriculum) contains sections on both theory and practice. The theoretical part of the curriculum is taught at the Berufsschule, while the practical part is the responsibility of the various businesses, industrial plants, and offices that participate in the program. Small businesses often join together to create a central training laboratory, where apprentices have access to a full range of training opportunities.

This combination of vocational schools and businesses makes up the "dual system." It trains young workers in Germany who start in a profession through a formal apprenticeship of about three years. This type of vocational training, which is concluded with a formal examination, produces highly skilled workers in more than 3,500 professions. Its origins, as discussed in Chapter 2, can be traced back to the early craft guilds that wanted to control the number and quality of personnel coming into a profession.

The concepts of present-day vocational education go back to Georg Kerschensteiner (1854-1932), a member of the German Reformpädagogik who was influenced by Pestalozzi. As mentioned in Chapter 2, Kerschensteiner worked as a superintendent at Munich and was heavily involved in vocational training. Since his time, vocational schools have been a central part of the German public school system. Nearly half of all students over the age of 16 are educated in vocational schools. The testing system of these schools is state-mandated but controlled by *Handwerkskammern* (chambers of crafts), which supervise the practical part of the curriculum. The businesses involved in the apprenticeships incur significant costs for their share in this form of education. Although apprenticeships are expensive for businesses, they accept these costs because they believe that vocational training of potential workers is an investment that ultimately will benefit their businesses.

Whereas the Gymnasium and Gesamtschule offer direct paths to higher education, in recent years students from vocational schools also have been able to pursue higher education — either in technical colleges or universities — as a later stage of their career development. In 1995 a law was passed that permits a *Meister* (a certified master craftsman) to begin higher education in a university. Because of this change, there now are two routes to higher education: the direct route through the college-bound tracks of the public schools — with the *Abitur* as the final qualification — and the indirect route through vocational training, apprenticeship, and continuing education. Although the second way gives the same exams and rewards, it is much more difficult than the first one and takes more time.

Recent economic problems have affected vocational education. In a time during which unemployment has risen to over 10%, not all businesses are willing to hire apprentices or to offer them a job after they are finished with their vocational training. Because the unemployment rate of young people has risen dramatically in the past few years, vocational schools are now retraining students who cannot find jobs in the fields for which they originally prepared. Therefore, vocational schools offer a large number of courses for continuing education in many areas to help students acquire new professional skills. In this respect, vocational schools not only are part of the public school system but also are an instrument to fight unemployment. While still a serious problem, youth unemployment in Germany ranks among the lowest in the European Community, well below neighboring France, Italy, and Denmark; and the vocational school initiatives are partially responsible.

The German "dual system" of vocational training has a good reputation and has been copied all over the world. But educators and politicians from other countries who want to "import" this system into their education systems sometimes ignore the fact that the German system is built on long-standing German and

European traditions, such as the self-regulation of the crafts and the understanding that training of workers is a responsible investment on the part of business and industry.

Conclusion

To complete this overview of German schools, the *Sonderschulen* for exceptional students need to be mentioned. Although in the past handicapped students were sorted out and sent to Sonderschulen for special education, today there is a movement to integrate students with special needs into the other schools as much as possible. There are not only advantages for the handicapped children, who grow up in a normal environment, but also for nonhandicapped students, who learn to accept and to work with handicapped students when they are integrated in the regular classroom.

Generally, all of the schools we have discussed are public schools operated and financed by the states. But in all tracks one can find private schools that are state-certified but not wholly state-supported. As state-certified schools, such private schools can receive up to 98% of their funding from the state. State law also permits private schools to exist that receive no public money or certification.

In spite of inroads made by the introduction of the "fourth track," the Gesamtschule, the traditional three-track system of education has a long history in Germany and appears to have a firm future. Indeed, sorting of students at the end of fourth grade is supported by 57% of Germans and opposed by only 32%.

CHAPTER FOUR

TEACHING AND LEARNING
IN GERMAN SCHOOLS

By law and tradition, German public schools are state schools. They are created, financed, organized, and supervised by the *Kultusministerien* (ministries of education) of the 16 different states, which, by the national constitution, are responsible for culture and education. The supervision is done locally by superintendents, who are civil servants appointed by the state.

Public schools are state agencies, and they are perceived as state agencies. This creates a reputation for solidity, stability, and reliability that results in an image of quality education. This perception is supported by the fact that most teachers are *Beamte* (civil servants) with tenure, who represent the state, and the fact that the curriculum is state-mandated. The state not only is formally responsible for the curriculum, the state controls it. Although teachers have the constitutionally guaranteed right to choose their own methods of teaching, the content is given to them. The state-given curriculum must be implemented. Teachers deliver all of the required themes and issues from the different subjects to the students. For a long time there was no discussion about whether students liked the state curriculum, whether it was important for the younger generation, or whether the teachers agreed with the curriculum that they were required to teach and students were required to learn. This required curriculum might be one of the reasons why German students, when they attend school in a foreign country, often do not have difficulty.

Not only does the state control schools through teachers and the curriculum, it also controls them by licensing teaching materials, including textbooks, films, audio cassettes, and computer software. Every textbook publisher must submit its textbooks to subject-based commissions that evaluate the textbooks to determine if they are in accordance with the curriculum of the state. Even the radio and television programs broadcast by public broadcasting companies and specifically produced for schools are supervised by a commission whose members are appointed by the state ministries of education. Computer programs and other electronic material produced for teaching purposes also are controlled by state commissions or institutes. Recently, some of these controls of instructional materials have been relaxed.

The right of students and parents to participate and co-determine education is regulated in the school laws of the 16 states. The parents of each class elect representatives as partners for consultation with the teachers and principals. These representatives, who may choose a speaker, are part of the school conference, which in some cases determines basic principles of school affairs that are administered by the principal. Usually the interest of the parents in elementary schools is greater than in secondary schools. It increases when the question arises about which secondary school a student should attend.

Curriculum

German schools place a high-level importance on the subject-based curricula and the acquisition of knowledge. The Gymnasium and Realschule in particular are known for the large amount of content that students are required to learn if they want to earn a final certificate, which will open the way to higher education and into certain professions. The Hauptschule and, since the 1970s, the Gesamtschule focus more on practical and social goals, such as developing craft skills, organizing one's learning processes, being able to work in teams, and communicating in public.

As a consequence of the subject-oriented teaching approach, students must learn six to 12 different subjects at the same time. Every school day is organized in different schedules, and the average lesson is 45 minutes.

The following tables illustrate typical schedules at the elementary and secondary levels.

Table 1. Grundschule, second grade (8 a.m. to 1 p.m. daily).

MONDAY	TUESDAY	WEDNESDAY	THURSDAY	FRIDAY
German	Math	German	Service	German
Math	German	Math	German	Math
Science	Catholic Religion	Fine Arts	Math	P.E.
Music	P.E.	Science	Catholic/ Protestant Religion	Fine Arts
P.E. for handicapped students				

Table 2. Realschule, ninth grade.

SUBJECT	LESSONS PER WEEK
German	4
Math	4
Religion	2
Geography	2
History	1
P.E.	2
Fine Arts	2
French	4
English	4
Physics	1
Biology	1
Chemistry	1
Optional Course	2

Table 3. Gymnasium, 12th grade.

TIME	MONDAY	TUESDAY	WEDNESDAY	THURSDAY	FRIDAY
8:00- 8:45	Fine Arts	History	French	Math	Chemistry
8:50- 9:35	Fine Arts	History	French	Math	Chemistry
9:50-10:35	French	English	Philosophy	German	Latin
10:40-11:25	French	English	Philosophy	German	Latin
11:40-12:25	Philosophy	Math	Latin	History	English
12:30-13:15	German	Math	Chemistry	French	Math
13:20-14:05		P.E.	Fine Arts	P.E.	

Shaded areas signify core or required courses at 12th grade.

Instruction and Evaluation

The focus on knowledge delivery instead of the training of abilities, particularly at the upper levels, has resulted in certain teaching approaches. Because the teacher is the main source of knowledge, the transmission of knowledge from the teacher to the student is the most common means of teaching. Research has found that 79% of the lessons in the Gymnasium, Hauptschule, and Gesamtschule are taught in a teacher-centered way, and cognitive goals were the focus more than 90% of the time (Hage et al. 1985).

The basic philosophy of the teacher-training programs and the teachers' views of themselves reinforce the notion that teachers are authorities in their subjects, rather than pedagogues. In the academic pecking order of public schools, the Gymnasium teacher is seen as the greatest knowledge authority and, therefore, traditionally has been the most respected. The place where student-centered approaches flourish is the elementary school, where an open classroom environment and a family-like atmosphere exist (Zahorik and Dichanz 1994).

German students are tested frequently. Basically, there are four different forms of testing: informal classroom tests, formal classroom tests, centralized subject tests, and special, formal tests.

Every teacher can — and is expected to — give informal classroom tests in every subject he or she teaches. The teacher is responsible for the content, the frequency, and the evaluation of these tests. Their main purpose is to evaluate the learning progress of the students. Twice a year the results of these classroom tests are summarized in an official report that is distributed to the students and their parents. The report is used in making decisions about future schooling at specific intervals: after the fourth, 10th, and 13th grades.

Most of these informal classroom tests are developed by teachers themselves to reflect the content they have taught in their lessons. In as many subjects as possible, teachers use an essay format, rather than multiple-choice or true-false, because German schools stress the ability of students to use their native language to express their learning and thinking. German teachers, on the whole, do not like to use commercially produced tests and other materials, because they do not want limits placed on their teaching autonomy.

The state curriculum in general does not regulate how to evaluate children. It merely requires a certain number of classroom tests each school year. The required tests vary from six to 10, depending on the subject.

Some of the 16 states require specific, formal classroom tests at certain times of a school year in primary subjects, such as German language, foreign languages, math, history, and science (biology, physics, chemistry, computer). In most cases the state mandates the number of tests, but not the content. These tests are evaluated and graded by the subject teacher according to state-established criteria so that the results can be compared across schools.

The most difficult test in a German student's career, perhaps in life, is the *Abitur*, a centralized subject test that serves as the final examination at the end of the Gymnasium. This test contains several essay questions in at least three subjects. The students have a half-day to write their answers. After they pass this written exam, students also are tested in a 30-minute oral exam in at least one additional subject by a committee of teachers at the school plus a supervisor from the Kultusministerien. These exams cover the complete content of the subject taught during the last three years.

In 1788 the Abitur was established as the only qualification to enter a university. Currently, it is a requirement for many professions in upper and upper-middle positions and a status symbol denoting that a good education has been achieved, as well as a university entrance requirement.

Special formal tests are used only to identify students with learning handicaps or special needs. Most of these tests are administered by school psychologists. Rarely are they administered by the teachers themselves.

In general, teachers in German schools rely on their observation of student performance and the results of informal tests, rather than on formal tests, when evaluating students. The use of standardized objective tests in German schools is quite limited, but there is a movement under discussion to use more objective tests, because parents and business people prefer clear judgments about students in terms of numbers and grades.

At the Elementary Level

Since the 1970s many teachers have moved toward more open teaching approaches that focus on the interests of the children to make learning more motivating and more effective. The Kultusminister has endorsed this movement and has issued new regulations that reduce the influence and specificity of the state curriculum and require schools to develop aspects of the school curriculum that are related to the particular environment of the school. The goals of these regulations are to make learning more concrete for students by using the community as a learning resource and to base learning at school on the conditions of real life, rather than on textbooks and other artificial learning resources.

Several other regulations that support the change of the teaching approach in elementary schools also have been issued. The four-year Grundschule is to be viewed as a unit of transition between the family and the public institution called "school."

Elementary classrooms are to be furnished and decorated "like living rooms," rather than merely as functional learning boxes. Generally, children are grouped at tables for four to six youngsters. There are shelves in the classroom with many learning materials. Several spaces with different functions, or learning centers, are present in almost all classrooms. These may include a reading corner, a rest area, an animal space, a science corner, and a computer niche. In addition to intensive learning activities in which children concentrate on specific instructional tasks, there are other activities, including storytelling and free learning, in which the children determine for themselves what to read and what to do.

The teacher has several functions in the student-centered learning approach. He or she is still the provider of knowledge and learning resources; but he or she also is the initiator and organizer, or the guide, who helps students to identify individual and group learning tasks. And the teacher is the counselor who talks to children about their concerns and anxieties.

Maintaining a stable class structure is very important in German elementary schools. Students often have the same classroom teacher for all four years of elementary school, except when they are taught by specialty teachers in such subjects as sports, religion, and music. All of the other subjects are taught by the classroom teacher, and this teacher also is the person who formulates the recommendation about which school track a child will follow on leaving the elementary school.

Elementary education has received a great deal of attention during the past 20 years. Many schools have experienced remarkable pedagogical reforms regarding teaching and learning. However, reform is ongoing. The 1995 National Conference on Elementary Education confirmed the current approach taken in today's elementary schools but also presented new guidelines, including:

- Teaching should not take place in traditional 45-minute periods. Instead, teachers should use the time between 8 a.m. and 1 p.m. according to the teaching and learning needs of children in a particular class.
- The relationship between teachers and students should mirror life in a democratic society. Neither the school as a state institution nor the teachers have "natural" authority. The school is to be seen as a community in which the people who live and work there determine principles concerning how to treat each other.
- Elementary schools should emphasize the goal of good health. This refers to nutrition as well as to sports activities and environmental awareness.
- Teachers should guide students to become independent, critical thinkers. Students need to experience themselves as parts of the real, surrounding world.

- Schools should offer opportunities for students to produce, use, and critically analyze media.

Today's elementary schools seek to demonstrate a new understanding of learning. Instead of the sterile delivery of knowledge, teachers try to catch students' interest and to motivate them to follow their personal curiosity as the main source for learning. Traditional learning skills, such as reading and math, are introduced where and when they are appropriate.

When a child leaves the elementary school at the end of the fourth grade to enter a Hauptschule, a Realschule, a Gesamtschule, or a Gymnasium, he or she faces several changes. In the secondary schools, content is organized into separate subjects, rather than in a holistic approach. Because different subjects are taught by different teachers, the children will meet many more teachers. And their new teachers will emphasize achievement and efficient learning more than their elementary teachers did. Their new teachers also will give more tests.

At the Secondary Level

The four secondary school tracks — Hauptschule, Realschule, Gesamtschule, and Gymnasium — favor different teaching and learning styles. The Hauptschule stresses concrete, practical knowledge, rather than analytical knowledge. The Realschule, a middle-level school, features languages, math, and basic professional skills.

The task of the Gesamtschule is as much social as it is cognitive. Therefore, one finds various means of learning in this type of school. In fact, the Gesamtschule is the track of German schools that experiments most in learning and teaching. It uses unusual ways to motivate students and to help them learn. Instead of adhering to the state curriculum, the Gesamtschule often develops its own curriculum. The basic pedagogical notion of the Gesamtschule is that it is more important to help students learn what is important to them, rather than to stress certain skills or

48

knowledge. Most innovations in teaching and learning in the last 20 years have come out of the Gesamtschule.

The Gesamtschule, after 25 years of existence, can be summarized as follows:

- The Gesamtschule, as a new type of school, is successful. Many Gesamtschulen have become true neighborhood schools, in contrast to other secondary schools.
- Communities have learned that a neighborhood school has many benefits for both the neighborhood and the school. They have recognized the Gesamtschule as a source of community identification and pride.
- Successful Gesamtschulen have become catalysts for school reform in general. Open schools, project teaching, school profiles, European schools, peace education, and social education emerged from the Gesamtschule and caused reforms and changes in the other secondary schools.

Finally, from its origin the Gymnasium has been the school that prepares students for the university. Although the Gymnasium is still a college preparatory school, it has begun to change in recent years. The proportion of children from elementary schools who enter the Gymnasium has increased in the last 10 years from 8% to 30%. This has caused many changes in traditional teaching and learning patterns, particularly in the teacher-centered approach and subject-matter focus. The Gymnasium is starting to adapt to the needs, abilities, and preconditions of its changing clientele.

The character of the state-controlled school, the status of the teachers as civil servants, and the teacher training programs combine to ensure a relatively stable school curriculum and a set of predictable teaching methods. There always has been a strong emphasis on subject-matter knowledge in all of the different subjects in the Gymnasium and Realschule, but both types of schools are beginning to take lessons from the Hauptschule and the Gesamtschule, which focus more on social-communicative abilities. The Gymnasium and Realschule are beginning to realize that the transmission of knowledge alone is insufficient to the future needs of their students. And neither students nor their parents will continue to accept a system that is bound only by tradition or state requirement. They expect schools and teachers to convince them about the usefulness of the current curriculum of these schools, and one consequence of this development is a demand for a more practical curriculum. Parents and students ask not only how well the school transmits knowledge, but also that a useful curriculum result in an up-to-date preparation for life.

Such expectations are difficult to fulfill for a school system that has had the same basic structure for 250 years. As part of the state bureaucracy, schools are not organized to react flexibly to new demands and developments. Likewise, the civil servant status of school personnel does not motivate teachers and supervisors to be creative and flexible. It is not surprising that many people believe the present German school system is outdated and needs a thorough reform. But, in fact, school reform has been a matter of the political discussion for many years, though little progress has been made (Deutscher Ausschuß 1959; Deutscher Bildungsrat 1970; Bildungskommission NRW 1995).

We will pursue this matter of school reform in a moment. But, because school reform includes the reform of teacher training, it will be useful to look at that area before proceeding.

Teacher Training

As in many other countries, teaching in Germany originally was done by priests, who were the only literate people of the time. Certainly by the beginning of the Enlightenment — and in many cases even earlier — both nobles and commoners were demanding more education; and the church could not stop various levels of government from starting their own schools with their own curricula. However, until about 1600 most teachers were not trained professionals. Indeed, many were hardly able to read or write themselves.

A number of teacher training institutions have been established since the opening of the 19th century, but the latest reform period is the most pertinent to this discussion. That took place in the 1960s, and since that time almost all teachers have been trained in universities. The basic state requirements for a certified teacher vary according to the intended teaching level. Teachers of the earlier grades are required to take somewhat more coursework in education, about 25% of their classes, compared to about 20% for teachers at the secondary level. And, of course, elementary and secondary teachers are distinguished according to their level of subject specialization, with elementary teachers taking a broader array of subjects.

In traditional fashion, the Gymnasium teachers see themselves as "scientists." In former times they were called "Professor," as they still are in Austria. They receive training at a university (just as other academic professions do) in one or two subjects. Pedagogical and psychological courses always were and still are a minor part of their curriculum. Students in teacher-training programs aimed at teaching in a Gymnasium receive subject-based training in scientific subjects and, indeed, are treated more like future scientists than future pedagogues.

After they are done with their university studies, the teachers need to pass a state examination in three subjects. On successful completion of the examination, they are eligible for the *Referendariat* (practical training), an introductory phase of 24 months, during which they practice-teach under the supervision of an experienced teacher with whom they meet in weekly seminars. After 24 months of training, these teachers must pass yet another state exam to become state-certified teachers and thus eligible to apply for a professional teaching position. (As of this writing, Germany is experiencing an oversupply of teachers, and only a few subjects offer many open positions each year.)

After teachers are appointed to positions by the Ministry of Education, they serve a probation of three years. During this time they are supervised by a local superintendent who evaluates their work. If everything is satisfactory, the teacher is granted tenure, which is for life. Once tenure is granted, teachers receive no other evaluations, nor are they required to engage in further education.

However, in most schools further education is expected, and teachers have many opportunities to continue their education through seminars and workshops that are offered by school districts, by the ministry itself, by the churches, and by political parties. A teacher who really wants to continue professional education in many cases will be allowed released time from teaching to attend training sessions, if the training is accredited by the Ministry of Education.

The social standing of teachers in Germany, particularly of Gymnasium teachers, is very high when compared to how teachers rank in many other countries. Teachers are viewed as key professionals in German society, ranking higher, according to polls, than such occupations as politicians and lawyers but somewhat lower than physicians, university professors, and priests.

School Finance

Although the school system is state-controlled, some responsibilities rest with the local communities. The communities are responsible for the physical preconditions for learning, such as providing school buildings, furniture, instructional materials, school maintenance, and student transportation. Because the communities receive school money from the general state tax in relation to student enrollments, there are no "rich" or "poor" schools. Sometimes, however, if there are high tax-paying businesses in a community, the school budget may be increased. Each company may provide additional financial support to public and private schools. Another factor that can cause differences among schools is parent organizations. They exist in every school. Also, there are statewide parent organizations for the different types of schools. These parent organizations influence state school policy. All of these factors can cause differences in the quality of education provided by schools, though they all are governed by the same set of state regulations.

In terms of expenditure of funds, schools are supervised very closely. They receive their yearly budgets from the community regardless of whether the budgets fit the schools' needs. From this perspective, schools are just like any other institution; they have little special autonomy. However, in a recent effort to save money, communities and states are giving more autonomy to the schools. The schools may receive a certain amount of money each year for their needs, but it is up to them to decide how they will use it. Schools also are allowed to look for sponsorships to support their work. Rather than provide paid positions for teachers, some state governments provide money for schools to spend as they see fit. Most of these regulations are quite new, and schools have not had a chance to take advantage of them. Therefore, it is not clear at the moment whether these regulations will result in creative and flexible use of funds.

School Reform

The current interest in school reform is reflected in teaching and learning research. Until the 1970s, research on teaching and learning was not a matter of scholarly interest. Now there are numerous studies concerning the reality of classroom teaching and learning. Individual schools are even asking for financial support to commission researchers to answer questions regarding daily life at school. Although teaching practice is heavily influenced by the general decline in funding for schools, interest in how to improve teaching and learning in schools is strong.

Although recently published official documents on school reform have suggested reforms in the basic structure, goals, and methods of schools, these reforms have not been widely implemented. The traditional patterns of teaching and learning persist. For example, one document urges changes related to 1) the understanding of life and learning in schools, 2) the responsibilities and administration of the schools, and 3) the definition of professionalism of teachers (Bildungskommission NRW 1995, p. xiii).

The traditional teacher-centered teaching and learning approach and the goal of delivering knowledge still characterize German schools, especially at the secondary level. However, reform is receiving much public support. Following is a summary of some key reforms that are starting to be seen:

- Because of the shrinking function of the family, the responsibilities of the school are growing and will grow further.
- As a school's responsibilities increase, the tasks of the teachers also increase. They are expected to do much more than in former times.
- Teachers need to recognize much more the differences in the socialization of children; teaching must be realized in an individualized and differentiated way.
- More parents want a longer school day. The school day ends at about 1 p.m., after 5 or 6 lessons. Sometimes there are optional working groups or extracurricular activities in the afternoon. In the last decade, as the interest of parents in leaving their children in school for the whole day is increasing, the number of schools offering an afternoon program for students has grown. Parents want their children to be supervised as long as they are not at home.
- Parents, business people, and educators expect that basic abilities, such as how to inform oneself, how to organize one's own learning, how to work in a team, and how to make decisions, are added to the traditional subject-based curriculum.
- Schools have started to recognize the learning needs and interests of their students. Instead of trying to fit the students to the schools, they fit the school to the students.
- Because of the importance of media in students' lives and in the economy, schools are beginning to teach basic computer skills, including the use of databases and the Internet.

Educators have asked for more flexibility to make schools more effective and learning more useful. The state has begun to accept this request and has given more autonomy to schools in terms of goals, content, and materials.

In the next chapter, we describe three case studies that illustrate typical schools and how they are dealing with both tradition and these new currents in German school philosophy and practice.

CHAPTER FIVE
THREE CASE STUDIES

This chapter contains three case studies that portray life in German schools. The three studies focus on Ludgeri Grundschule (an elementary school), Max Planck Gymnasium (a college preparatory high school), and Hasperg Gesamtschule (a comprehensive high school). They are based on personal observations, discussions with teachers, and documents available in the schools.

Ludgeri Grundschule

Ludgeri Grundschule is located in Rheine, a city of about 35,000 inhabitants in northwest Germany. One of nine municipal elementary schools, Ludgeri Grundschule is a denominational mid-size elementary school with about 260 students and 13 full- and part-time teachers. The number of foreign children is about 1%, most of whom immigrated from the former socialist states of the Soviet Union and Poland. The parents of the students have average incomes; several are teachers themselves. The school district is one of the older ones in this city; the inhabitants are settled; the environment is orderly and clean. Many families own their houses. There are few social problems in the area; most people have jobs; the unemployment rate is below average. Most of the mothers do not work outside of the home.

Most municipal elementary schools are nonreligious in this city. Protestant and Islamic parents so far have not requested Protestant or Islamic elementary schools, though schools of these denominations do exist in other cities. In the case of Ludgeri Grundschule, the Catholic Church, St. Ludgeri, and its priests and parishioners play an important role — both in the school and in the neighborhood. Because of the strong belief in the Catholic faith of most of the population in this particular part of the town, this public school has been constituted as a Catholic elementary school. This is possible and legal when parents desire it.

The Ludgeri Grundschule comprises grades 1 through 4, as do all elementary schools in Germany. Students are grouped into eight classes. Each class has its own classroom, where the students remain for the school day, which begins at 8 a.m. and ends at 1 p.m. Lessons are taught by the classroom teacher with the exception of music, sports, and religion, which are taught by special teachers. The students in a given class have the same classroom teacher and are kept as an intact group, as much as possible, for the entire four years of elementary school. This creates a family-like atmosphere that eases the home-to-school transition. Because of the depth of familiarity between the teacher and the students and among the students, formal rules and regulations are unnecessary and few discipline problems arise. Foreign visitors often are surprised at the informal functioning of the class and the willingness and readiness of the students to be responsible, self-directed, and concerned for others. Learning activities differ from teacher to teacher, from subject to subject, and from day to day. Elementary teachers have a lot of freedom regarding how to teach. They may lead some lessons and have the students work as groups in others.

On a recent morning Mrs. Munten, a 52-year-old teacher, guided her class of second-graders into their classroom, the room in which they began the first grade. Mrs. Munten and her students have made the room a very comfortable and productive learning environment. It contains a reading corner with soft chairs, a math corner with many learning materials, a science area with a fish aquarium and a cage with two marmots, and a play and rest area for relaxation. The walls and the closets are decorated with children's posters and paintings. The teacher's desk, located in a corner, is loaded with textbooks, paper, pens, and boxes. The atmosphere is orderly, but also creative and flexible. It is similar to the idea of the *Wohnstube* (living room) that educators such as Pestalozzi and Petersen proposed for classrooms.

Mrs. Munten's class includes 26 students, who are organized in groups of four to six students in a desk cluster with two students at each desk. Because this is second grade, the students already know what to do. As Mrs. Munten starts the school day with a morning circle, students tell about their experiences of the previous day and evening, what they found exciting, what problems they encountered, and so forth. This discussion gives Mrs. Munten the chance to know something about what her students have been doing, to hear about their concerns and joys, and to find connections between the children's experiences and the curriculum. She has outlined a workplan for the week on the chalkboard. Without any delay, some students start working on math exercises in their math books. Others start with materials on local history that the teacher has prepared.

One group begins to discuss how to organize a project on ways to clean rainwater for drinking purposes. This group determines questions to be answered, ways to do experiments with sieves and filters, and how to report about their work to the class. A group of three sits in a corner and starts reading stories aloud to each other. After a little while, the teacher stops this period of individual learning and calls for attention. She wants to introduce a new operation in math, which she needs to explain to the whole class. After the introduction, a math exercise is assigned that is to be finished by break time.

After a short break, the children listen to a story about birds told by the teacher. Students are asked to summarize the story in their own words. Some do it in a group while others work on their own. Many ask the teacher questions while she walks through the class. The teacher offers support and counsel to children who need it. There is no lecturing. After 40 minutes and another short break, Mrs. Munten asks the children to form a line in front of her desk. She places a drop of perfume on each student's hand and sends them back to their seats. Then on the board she writes the following question: "Why does perfume smell so nice and intense?" The students have 15 minutes to work on this question in their groups. They raise and discuss additional questions, compare perfume with water, and look up additional information in an encyclopedia and other sources. After the groups are finished with their work, Mrs. Munten asks for reports from each group. Finally, she and the students together summarize solutions, and she writes them on the board. The students write the solutions in their notebooks.

Now, after two hours of work, the students are ready for their "breakfast" (a morning snack) break. Some teachers prefer to let the children go outside, while others prefer that they have breakfast in the classroom. Mrs. Munten understands the importance of a cozy breakfast together with her students as a way to develop social skills in the classroom community. After the 10-minute breakfast, the children go outside to the playground.

While the students take their playground break, the teachers convene in the staff room for coffee. Following the break, the school day continues, and Mrs. Munten begins another math lesson. At the beginning of this math period, she gives information and writes an explanation on the chalkboard. Afterward, students solve problems that Mrs. Munten has prepared at home. The problems consist of three packages, each with five tasks of increasing difficulty. Two additional tasks are narrative problems that the students must answer in words rather than equations.

Each student works alone but sits with his or her group. The class is quiet, though some students confer with each other. At the end of the math lesson, Mrs. Munten collects the work and assigns other problems that the students will work on at home. These problems deal with the topic introduced today in class, but the problems are at different ability levels. For more able students there are three narrative problems that require math understanding, an identification of the math problem, and an independent solution.

According to the structure that a teacher gives the class, there might be much movement during the school day, and the teacher may function more as a guide and facilitator. In science, for example, students organize themselves and work independently; the teacher merely monitors the learning.

Besides daily lessons in which the children learn specific subjects, the teacher may assign long-term projects. Also, the teacher may engage students in outdoor activities or invite other people into the classroom to make learning more motivating. At the end of the year, however, the teacher will be responsible for ensuring that the requirements of the state curriculum are fulfilled.

For the last hour of the day, between noon and 1 p.m., Mrs. Munten leaves her class to teach religion to another class, because she is one of the few teachers on the staff who is certified by the Catholic Church to teach religion. While she is away, the sports teacher enters the class to teach physical education. After an hour of play and exercises in which the students climb over and crawl under obstacles, roll a ball through a labyrinth, and jump over their classmates, the school day is over.

Most students walk home on their own because they live close by, but others are driven home as part of a mothers' car pool. As the students leave, Mrs. Munten goes to the staff room, where the principal is about to hold a staff meeting. After the meeting Mrs. Munten and the other teachers also can go home. Most of them live in the village where the school is located, but others drive in from neighboring towns.

Mrs. Shulz, the principal, is not finished with her work. She is expected at the superintendent's office at 3 p.m. to meet other principals to discuss opportunities for school collaboration as an economy measure. The school district superintendent has announced that there might be another budget reduction next year, and he has asked the principals to find creative ways to conserve resources.

Once the children arrive at home, they are ready for homework and leisure activities. Many curriculum elements that are part of the elementary school experience in the United States, such as co-curricular activities, are not routinely included in German schools. Thus the longer afternoon away from school allows students and their parents time to take on these activities. Some have private lessons in music or art, others enjoy sports and join the many children's groups in the different local *Vereine*, or sports clubs, that organize leisure sports. Some children play outdoors in park areas available in the neighborhood.

Max Planck Gymnasium

When foreigners talk about the German school system and the quality of German education, they usually are referring to the Gymnasium and its goals, curriculum, teaching and learning methods, and high expectations. Although the Gymnasium is only one of the four types of schools in the German secondary system — and usually considered the most elite type — it is now attended by about 30% of the high school students. The Max Planck Gymnasium is an interesting case, because it is located in the former East Germany.

The Gymnasium, as a school type, is widely respected. Therefore, East German parents chose the Gymnasium as the model to restructure one of the former comprehensive schools in the state of Thüringen. To understand how this type of school functions — and the principal problems of this particular school — one needs to consider the political situation in the new Eastern states of Germany. The transformation of a former DDR school into a West German-style Gymnasium as a consequence of reunification reveals characteristics of this type of school, as well as some of the ongoing difficulties of the reformation of traditional schools and their infrastructures.

Before describing life in a Gymnasium in the former DDR, it is necessary to examine the origins of this particular Gymnasium itself in the former East Germany. The Max Planck Gymnasium is located in Chemnitz, a mid-sized city in Thüringen, the southernmost state in the former East Germany. This city of 200,000 inhabitants is a former industrial metropolis that has lost 80% of its former plants and businesses to two neighboring cities, Dresden and Leipzig. Many men and women have lost their jobs; the unemployment rate was 30% and is only now slowly decreasing. It will take decades to rebuild the labor market, and there is much uncertainty about the people and the politicians in this area. Consequently, the schools play a very important role in this economic environment. They can prepare students for the new jobs that will be developed, and they can keep students off the street while they are unemployed.

During the actual process of the reunification, parents were curious to learn about the opportunities provided to students in the Western school system with its four tracks. They were used to a comprehensive system. Some schools, such as EOS (*Erweiterte Oberschule*), offered the chance to qualify for a technical college or a university. Other schools, such as the POS (*Polytechnische Oberschule*), could not do so.

Parents of students who attended (or would attend) the previous incarnation of the Max Planck school, then a POS, learned from other parents and politicians that the Gymnasium was the most attractive type of Western school they could choose. Therefore, in a school conference they decided to restructure their school into a Gymnasium. They did not know much about this type of school, its goals, methods, or requirements; but they had heard about its reputation, and they wanted the best education for their children. At the time of the formal reunification of Germany, there was no authorized school administration in the new states to approve of this decision; but many teachers at the school agreed to, or at least accepted, the desire of the school conference to change the school. They looked for help and support in the Western states from relatives, friends, colleagues, union members, school administrators, and politicians. And the Western states decided to support the democratic development in the East by sending trained personnel to provide assistance. In fact, when the city asked for support in its effort, a southern German city sent Mr. Gauss, a 42-year-old experienced Gymnasium teacher, to serve as a temporary principal at what was to become the Max Planck Gymnasium.

Mr. Gauss had never been to Chemnitz before, he had never seen an Eastern school, had not met the staff, and had not met the students or their parents. He understood his assignment in the East as a political and pedagogical challenge.

When Mr. Gauss left his school in southern Germany in the fall of 1990 and arrived to begin his work at the Max Planck Gymnasium, he faced many problems in addition to those that every principal has to master. Some of the specific start-up problems included:

- No valid school law in the newly "Westernized" state.
- No specific agreement about the Gymnasium as a type to be replicated.
- An existing school run by a committee of volunteers, a so-called roundtable, that included parents, teachers, and the principal.
- Many current teachers unqualified to teach in a Gymnasium.
- No decision about which students would be eligible to attend the new school.
- No determination regarding whether the curriculum requirements and electives — as determined by the roundtable — would be sufficient for the Gymnasium diploma, the *Abitur*, or university entrance qualification.

By 1996, most of these problems were overcome, and the Max Planck Gymnasium had become an ordinary (Section II) school for advanced students (Tillmann 1993; Weishaupt and Zedler 1994). With its 1,150 students, it is slightly above average in size. The staff includes 96 teachers (36 women and 60 men), 21 of whom teach part time. Among the part-time teachers there also are a Protestant minister and two Catholic priests, who teach religion as part of the normal curriculum. For physical education, music, and fine arts, there are special teachers. Most other teachers teach two subjects, depending on their qualifications. Their regular teaching load is between 26 and 21 hours, depending on their age and some extra tasks in the school administration. During the school day they move from class to class while the students stay in the same classroom all day, except when they are taught in the gym, a laboratory, or the music hall.

The student schedule changes from day to day. Every 45 minutes another teacher will enter a room, and the subject is changed. Sometimes a teacher stays for two lesson hours, but normally a student faces five or six different teachers for different subjects every morning. The school day will be finished between 1 p.m. and 2 p.m. Only 12th- and 13th-grade students have some lessons in the afternoon. But the students have many homework assignments, and so an average learning day may well be eight to 10 hours long.

The traditional Gymnasium of the past embodied a philosophy that said, in essence, that success was up to the student. This highly teacher-centered approach has given way in modern times to teachers taking on greater responsibility for their students' success. This change was brought about by the changing expectations of the parents and changes in the political environment for education — changes that also have meant a rise from 8% to 30% in the proportion of high school students attending the Gymnasium.

Students in a Gymnasium attend for nine years. In the first three years they have only mandatory classes, no electives. They start with one foreign language (either English or Latin) and continue to French, Italian, Spanish, or ancient Greek in the fourth year. In the fourth or fifth year the school starts to offer elective courses to the students, who then can choose between basic or advanced courses in many subjects. (Actual subjects taught vary among schools.) To earn the Abitur, students are required to pass a certain number of classes in subjects required by the state Ministry of Education.

Let us follow Heike, a 15-year-old girl who attends 5th level (11th grade) at the Max Planck Gymnasium through a typical day. Because she and her parents live in a village 10 miles east of the school, she has to get up early. The school bus leaves at 7:10, and so she must leave the house at 7 a.m. On the bus Heike chats with her classmates about the previous day. But for half of the bus trip she also practices the French vocabulary that she was expected to learn at home.

Heike enters the school at 8 a.m. The first lesson is German language, taught by Mr. Beyer, an experienced teacher about 50 years old. His teaching is quite traditional. He starts the lesson by repeating the rules of grammar from the previous lesson. Then he gives a presentation of the content to be learned today, asks the students to complete exercises in the textbook, and checks the students' work while they are writing. Shortly before the end of the lesson, Mr. Beyer gives a test. He collects the tests after the students are done and takes them home to correct them.

When Mr. Beyer leaves the class, Mrs. Nellen comes for the French lesson. Students change their books, chat, and laugh. Mrs. Nellen is a vivacious individual and begins a conversation in French to draw the attention of the class. She reports on the French Open Tennis Tournament that took place last weekend. She asks questions, plays word games, uses a news article for reading exercises, and, in general, tries to give the lesson a French-like atmosphere. At the end of the lesson, Mrs. Nellen and the class plan a French breakfast of croissants, café au lait, and baguettes for a future day.

After the French lesson there is a mid-morning "breakfast" break of 20 minutes. The students leave the classroom to walk around, to have a snack, and to meet their friends. Heike looks for the girls from her village to make plans. She has joined a swimming club and wants do some training in the afternoon.

As the girls return to class at the end of the break they groan because they anticipate the arrival of Mr. Paulsen, a lively young math teacher who demands a lot of them. Mr. Paulsen starts the math lesson with exercises in fractions. Groups of three students sit together and find and solve fraction problems. After this warm-up Mr. Paulsen calls for attention and tells the class a story that contains a math problem. The students must identify, formulate, and solve this problem. In groups of four to six students, they write the math problem in their own words and find their solutions. At the end of the lesson, the teacher can identify seven different descriptions of the same math problem and three different solutions that are all correct.

Mr. Paulsen leaves the room, and Mrs. Gruender comes in to teach social studies. Mrs. Gruender is very much engaged in social activities. She has developed a school program to give students the chance to experience social responsibility. She has organized such practica for the 11th-graders for many years. Her task today is to inform her students about the institutional conditions of some day-care centers for adults who need permanent support. Heike will have the chance to work in a house with mentally retarded children during her practicum. And so she asks many questions about the house and the duties she can expect. Several students will work in similar institutions; therefore, Mrs. Gruender takes the time for intensive explanation. At the end of the lesson she talks about the goal and the potential content of the report that the students will have to write about their practicum.

After another short break the students start their last period of the school day. During this period boys and girls are separated for a two-hour physical education program. While Mrs. Stein teaches the girls in the gym, Mr. Thomas walks with the boys to a community swimming pool nearby for swimming instruction. Both groups start with some warming up before they continue with their special training. At the end of these lessons, both groups also get the chance for some free play; the girls play volleyball, while the boys race one another across the swimming pool.

At 1:30 p.m. the school day is over, and the students, including Heike, leave the school. She rides the bus and is back home by 2:20 to have lunch. Before she starts her swimming training in the local municipal pool, Heike does her homework in French and biology. In the evening she plans to read her German assignment for the next day.

Most of the teachers leave the school by early afternoon. Only the fine arts teacher and the chemistry teacher stay, because they work with a special group in an elective subject. Mr. Linden, the principal, has a conference with two of his deputies and the counselor to discuss how to prepare the 12th-graders for the transition to the university after their 13th year. In the evening he also will have two meetings with parents to discuss outdoor activities for classes.

Heike, at age 15, is too young to know what she wants to do after high school. She might go into foreign languages as an interpreter or become a teacher, because she likes foreign languages. But nobody has reliable data about the labor market five years ahead on which to base any firm plans. However, Heike can be sure that the Abitur, the prestigious Gymnasium diploma, will give her the best chance for a job or for further education. The Abitur is the entrance ticket for every mid- or upper-level position, and so she is quite confident about her future.

Hasperg Gesamtschule

The Hasperg Gesamtschule, located in Hagen, is one of the types of German secondary schools that were built beginning in the 1960s, when the Social Democrats were in office in the state of North Rhine-Westphalia. The goal of the Gesamtschule was to offer equal educational opportunity for every child, especially for those from working-class families. Thus the Gesamtschule was unique in comparison to the other types of German schools, which had a role in "sorting" students according to their class, family, and academic backgrounds and their presumed future careers.

Georg, one of three children in his family, whose father works as a truck driver, can take advantage of this particular school. While he attended elementary school, his grades were only average. He did not like reading and writing very much. He barely got along in math. But whenever there was a task that called for experimentation or critical thinking, he excelled. In organizing group activities, play, competitions, and so on, he was engaged, effective, and accepted by his classmates. His parents could not help him because of their limited education and lack of time, and so they decided to send him to the Gesamtschule for two reasons: 1) The Gesamtschule is known for its efforts to teach every student regardless of his or her talents, and 2) it differentiates in what it offers. In addition, the Hasperg Gesamtschule is a Ganztags-schule, a school that takes care of the children from 8 a.m. to 4 p.m.

Georg, 16 years old, is unlike Heike in the previous case, as he is a 9th-grader. But he feels at home at his school, which he has attended for five years. Although his grades still are only average, he is accepted by his classmates and the teachers. He has become part of the "school establishment" because he is involved in many activities inside and outside the classroom. Many students and teachers like him because of his friendliness, his open character, and his reliability. He is the student speaker of his class and a member of the student council; he is involved in the canoe club and a Third World group that supports a school in Nepal. And he takes part in two study projects for the school. One deals with environmental protection of the area in which the school is located, and the other supports the assistance and integration of children from refugee families living in a temporary camp nearby. In addition to all of his school-related activities, which keep him busy all day long, he finds time to meet friends for roller skating, to listen to music, and to go to parties.

We can examine a day in Georg's life and find, on a typical school day, that he has quite a mixed program. He starts with a two-hour written exam in German. He must recall the content of a short story that he had to read at home the previous evening. In addition, he must describe one of the main characters of the story. This is quite a challenge for him, because he is not skillful at expressing his thoughts. But he wants, at least, to demonstrate to the teacher that he has read the story.

After the test and a short break, the class is combined with another, and the students are subdivided into groups of the same religious belief. Georg's parents are Catholic, which puts him into the group that is taught by Father Meyer, a local priest who serves the community as well as teaching school. During the religion lesson the students discuss the question of what it means to be a foreigner in a society, both for the foreigner and for the society and community that host the foreigner.

The succeeding lesson also is a discussion. The students are preparing a project that they will undertake with the supervision of their classroom teacher, Mr. Schulz. They will take a three-day outdoor excursion on bicycles this summer, and they need to prepare now. Where do they want to go? Where can they sleep? What food should they take? What route will be best? Who will be responsible for first aid? Who will repair the bicycles? When the bell rings, the students have collected many questions but few answers. They will need several more hours of preparation before the project will be ready.

In the fifth and sixth hours the students have a guest in the classroom. Mr. Kummel, from the local drug-prevention office, provides information about the local and national drug scene and answers the students' questions about drugs. The students quickly realize that Mr. Kummel is an honest and open man who really wants to inform them. He answers their questions candidly, and so the students feel free to ask him many questions.

After a demanding morning of six class hours, the students break for lunch, which is prepared in the school kitchen. They relax, chat, and have a walk outside until they assemble in the classroom again about 2 p.m. Mr. Schulz, the classroom teacher, is in charge of social studies. In combination with the bicycle project mentioned above, he starts to discuss advantages and disadvantages of different ways of traveling. This is part of the preparation for the project, but it also is a lesson about environmental protection. The class has to do some investigation as homework for social studies.

For the last lesson of the day, the students are greeted by Mrs. Hind. The subject is English.

Because Georg knows that his parents are not yet at home when the school day ends, he takes his rollerblades and skates to a meeting place in the city park. There he also meets comrades from other schools; they all like to skate, talk, and smoke cigarettes together. He stays about an hour before he leaves for home to have something to eat and to see his mother and his sisters. Even then, his father is still on the road with his truck. Georg will not see him today.

It has been a long day, and Georg is not sure that he will have the energy to do the math homework for the next day, but he knows that he ought to do the work.

On the whole Georg and his parents are quite pleased with the Hasperg Gesamtschule and its education. The school gives Georg a chance to experience progress and to develop self-esteem. He is not one of the most able students. But he likes to engage in group work, he is reliable, and he is friendly. Teachers like him because he supports group activities and because he is creative in organizing extracurricular work. Other types of schools might not recognize these qualities, because they focus only on academics; and so Georg would not have a good chance in those schools. But because the Gesamtschule stresses social learning, people like Georg get a chance at the kind of education that works best for them. Many businesses around the Hasperg Gesamtschule like to hire students from this particular school as apprentices, because the students usually are reliable and willing to work. So Georg will have a good chance of finding a satisfactory job when he leaves school next year, after the 10th grade. Only about 40% of his classmates will continue on to another school to earn the Abitur, which will make them eligible to attend a college or university or to take a middle-level position in the labor market.

The success of the Gesamtschule is not in doubt, especially after an intensive evaluation — the most extensive of any German school type ever (Fend 1982). However, it is not accepted as a regular public school in all of the German states. It was founded by Social Democrats in the states they controlled at that time, and it still suffers from this political "taint." Therefore, regardless of its educational success, which research supports, its future is uncertain.

The last two cases, in particular, exemplify the nature of the German school experience. If one remembers the history of the German school system (as discussed in Chapter 2), then it is not difficult to understand that the three traditional types of schools even today represent the social structure of Germany. There always have been attempts to put together children of different backgrounds into one comprehensive school system. Such well-known pedagogues as Comenius, Pestalozzi, and Humboldt have strongly advocated the idea of a comprehensive school, but without success. When the German parliament of the Weimar Republic met in 1918, the Socialists and other parties tried to found a comprehensive school system. The parliament accepted only a compromise that brought together children of all families into a comprehensive *elementary* school (grades 1 to 4). All the other types of schools remained the same.

This structure has not yet changed. The experiment of the Gesamtschule as the one unifying, comprehensive type of secondary school has not been politically successful. Instead of replacing three different, socially discriminating types of schools by just one, it has been added as a fourth type. Some observers believe that the

German system thus has become even more differentiated — and thereby more suitable to students with different needs and ambitions. But others believe that the addition of the Gesamtschule merely has stabilized the system through minor, rather than major reform; and so the differentiated system serves as a mirror of the German society and its social selection processes.

CHAPTER SIX
THE FUTURE:
PROBLEMS AND PROMISE

The experiment to establish the Gesamtschule as a comprehensive school can be regarded as the last attempt in this century to change the fundamental structure of the German three-track school system. This experiment, though pedagogically successful, has largely failed in the political arena. Today one can hardly find a politician who would dare to discuss or become involved in issues related to the basic structure of the German school system. In fact, many of the experiments to reform the German school system disappeared with the end of the 1980s. The Rau commission, an independent commission appointed by Johannes Rau, governor of North Rhine-Westphalia, found that during the 1970s and 1980s a fundamental change in the education work of the single school could not be reached (Bildungskommission NRW 1995, p. xi). Even the opportunities to rebuild the school system in the new states that resulted from the reunification of Germany after 1990 were not taken (Weishaupt and Zedler 1994). Indeed, nearly the reverse occurred: The old school system of the DDR was adapted to the traditional West German system with some minor changes. For historical and social reasons many characteristics of the old system still continue (Tillmann 1994).

The unwillingness of politicians, educators, and parents to consider reform of the existing school system is not a new phenomenon. Since 1948, when the Federal Republic of Germany was founded, several committees of the federal administration have been charged with examining education policies. In 1953 the "Deutscher Ausschuß für das Erziehungs- und Bildungswesen" was constituted as an independent committee to reform the German school system. Then in the 1970s a couple of reform initiatives were suggested. The "Deutscher Bildungsrat" was created to study education. It published the *Strukturplan für das Bildungswesen*, an important pedagogical document. But the plan did not have much effect, though it was widely discussed by administrative educators and scholars. In 1973 another committee of federal and state authorities released the "Bildungsgesamtplan," a political compromise between the federal government and the states. But that plan also made little difference in the traditional system.

Today there are no reform committees. Whenever any policy documents are released, they are generated by either a political party, associations of education professionals, or scholars. The discussion of education issues is highly ideological because of the interest in education of various political groups in German society. Education is guided, for the most part, by two committees of administrators: the "Ständige Konferenz der Kultusminister," a permanent committee of the Ministry of Education of the independent states, and the "Bund-Lander Kommission," a permanent committee to coordinate politics, reforms, and regulations between the federal government and the state governments. At best, these committees justify their politics; but they do little reflection on or planning for the future.

Current Issues

At present a number of education issues are being widely discussed in Germany. These include student motivation, the needs of youth, teacher dissatisfaction, the role of the family, the effect of electronic media, and shrinking school budgets.

Student motivation. As discussed in Chapter 2, the main focus of German schools traditionally has been teaching content. Teachers are expected to teach as much content knowledge as possible. This approach is being questioned today for several reasons. Because of the increasing amount of knowledge that is being created, the set curriculum of the schools tends to be increasingly outdated. Students have begun to see that the information they learn at school often is out of date and thus of little worth. They become bored by such content and look elsewhere for stimulation.

Students also recognize that their teachers often do not know what interests students and what they want to learn, because the teachers have been so focused only on content. Therefore, many students are not motivated to learn or to follow the approaches of their teachers. As a consequence, many teachers have become frustrated by their students' apparent lack of willingness to learn. Problems related to courtesy and discipline rank high in polls of students, teachers, and parents.

The needs of youth. The motivation issue is closely related to the perceived inability of the schools to meet the needs of the younger generation. Students complain about the content they are required to learn because it is not useful content. Businesses complain that students are not prepared for the labor market because the students exit schools with limited practical skills. Colleges and universities complain that students lack basic academic skills and learning-to-learn skills, such as how to organize and plan, how to find information on their own, and how to be responsible. And parents complain that schools have not really taken on the task of comprehensive education, as families become less able to provide for their children's education in areas traditionally left to families.

School funding levels also are under attack. Ministers and politicians complain that they have doubled or tripled the amount of money spent on education compared to 20 years earlier, but the achievement of students is lower today than it was two decades ago. And so the schools have been criticized for poor use of finances and personnel. The critics say that schools need to be run more like businesses. The recommendations about how to change schools are as endless as the problems the schools are expected to solve.

Teacher dissatisfaction. For many years the authority of the teacher was supreme. Teachers were seen as subject-matter experts charged with educating students so that the students gained the necessary knowledge and skills to function successfully in school, at work, and even within the family. In addition, teachers were authorities by law. As civil servants, they were representatives of the state.

But today the authority of teachers is being questioned. If young people believe that the knowledge and skills they are expected to acquire are not important, that what they learn at school is outdated and will not guarantee them a future job, then their respect for teacher authority is diminished and problems arise. Teachers feel the effects of this questioning of their efficacy, and the problems increase teacher dissatisfaction with their own careers.

A compounding factor has been the proliferation of computers and network accessibility. The school has lost its monopoly on the dispensing of knowledge and skills.

Finally, there now is a national debate about whether teachers should continue to be employed as civil servants. Clearly, teaching is no longer the comfortable, prestigious job that it once was in Germany, even though German teachers still enjoy a higher reputation than do teachers in many other countries.

The role of the family. The shift of education from families to schools has been ongoing for decades, but the erosion of parental influence is greatly accelerating at this time. Because of the demands of their children, many parents have, in essence, resigned from their responsibilities. They do not set limits to their children's consumption demands. Also, they are unsure about the goals for their children, particularly in terms of values. Guidance from the churches, political parties, state government, and other institutions is often limited. And parents of today's young people follow the lifestyle developed by the society in general.

Furthermore, as in other parts of the Western world, families are becoming smaller. Many are headed by only one adult. And family homes are becoming emptier, as more women (42% in 1996) work outside the home than ever before. Many of the functions that families used to perform are now the responsibility of the schools. This causes school adjustments and, as mentioned in the previous section, contributes to teacher dissatisfaction.

The effect of electronic media. Former Bundespräsident Richard von Weiszäcker called for a national study of the impact of electronic media on education. The study, *Bericht zur Lage des Fernsehens*, was released in 1995 and resulted in new guidelines to

78

promote media education in public schools. Many conferences, workshops, and committees now are dealing with the question of how to make media education more effective and how to motivate teachers and schools to improve their media use. As a result, for example, the state of North Rhine-Westphalia has started a project called "Schulen ans Netz" (Schools on the Internet), in which the school administration, media companies, and foundations are collaborating to improve media education.

Shrinking school budgets. In Germany, as in many other industrialized countries with a high standard of social services, the public money available for education is being reduced. Public schools, vocational schools, universities, and on-the-job-training programs all are suffering from shrinking funds. One of the few exceptions is the initiative to enhance media education, which was mentioned above.

These problems, though serious and in most cases not unique to Germany, do not represent a complete picture of where German schools may be headed. The current successes of German education show more of the direction the future may hold. Thus it will be useful to look not just at current issues that pose problems but also at the promises that modern German education holds for the future.

Promise

When critics, politicians, educators, parents, and business leaders realized that the traditional three-track system of German schools was not amenable to change because of political reasons, reform efforts began to be refocused. Three areas of reform have been identified: reorganizing school administration, changing school financing, and changing basic pedagogical assumptions and approaches.

Reorganizing school administration. School administrators, teachers, and education experts agree that it has become increasing unwieldy — and in some cases, impossible — to deal effectively with school problems through the traditional, centralized structure of school administration at the state level. According to school research from all over the world, it is the single school where reforms need to be initiated and operationalized (Berg and Steffens 1991; Effective Schools 1983). The principal, the teachers, the students, and the parents must direct school reform. Therefore, reform plans and proposals now are directed at the school site as the most important reform unit. It is now generally accepted that the centralized structure of school administration has not been effective, and state control needs to be reduced.

Most states today use a three-level structure of school administration: 1) the Ministry of Education as part of the state government, 2) the *Regierungspräsidenten* as a middle-level administration under the supervision of the state government, and 3) the superintendents of schools as the local authorities who act in the name of the ministry. Many experts are convinced that the three levels of administration are not needed and that the administrative structure should be collapsed (Liket 1993). They propose that the responsibilities of the local superintendent be split and that some of them be given to the school principal and some of them be given to the middle-level administration. Many critics, in fact, see superintendents as obstacles to reform efforts in the schools.

As the most important reform unit, the individual schools are being encouraged to develop initiatives on their own in the areas of curriculum development, school evaluation, and teacher training. Schools are being encouraged to develop specific profiles or programs, in which they differ from other schools, in order to meet the needs of their actual students, not "students" in the theoretical sense. To facilitate these initiatives, some states have reduced the required curriculum lesson hours by as much as 50%, so that schools can develop a curriculum that uniquely suits their school. Some state programs of teacher training also are being reduced, and schools are organizing their own teacher training to meet educational needs as they are determined by the school.

Changing school financing. Many communities have changed their financial regulations and given the principal the opportunity to spend school money as the school conference wishes to spend it. Even in terms of hiring and firing personnel, the principal in some communities has become the deciding authority, rather than the community or the state. Many schools have taken this freedom and initiated important changes. The motivation to give schools more autonomy is based not only on pedagogical arguments. Many communities that have given schools more freedom also have reduced the money budgeted for the school. For this reason, not all principals are enthusiastic about the change.

An example of the trend to give schools more autonomy is a regulation in North Rhine-Westphalia, called *Geld statt Stellen* (money instead of positions). Based on the number of students in each school, the school receives a certain amount of state money and can spend it as it chooses, such as for teachers, for additional personnel, for special projects, or for equipment. With this procedure, the state not only gives more financial autonomy to the single school, it also saves money.

Because of tight budgets, schools are encouraged by the state to search for sponsors to support various activities. Although commercial advertising in the schools still is banned and the idea is not popular in Germany, the opposition to advertising is beginning to weaken.

Although there are many opportunities for change and the future is bright, many communities maintain the status quo. They still accept the old arrangement in which communities are responsible for the buildings, equipment, and nonteaching personnel, but the state controls the goals and curriculum of the schools. In general, one can observe that the character of schools as official state institutions is changing. State control of schools is loosening, and the view is increasing that schools should be self-governing institutions with the right to determine their own goals. This trend is beginning to cause competition among secondary schools and the acceptance of more evaluation.

Changing basic pedagogical assumptions and approaches. Related to the preceding are many pedagogical changes that are occurring in German schools. These changes include a new legitimation of the school as an institution, a different understanding of the learning process, a student-centered instructional approach, a new definition of the teacher's function, an effort to make schools more "effective," and new requirements for evaluation of both individual teachers and the school in general. According to a recent poll by the Gewerkschaft Erziehung und Wissenschaft (the teachers union), 80% of the secondary school teachers support the idea of more independence for schools, 90% agree with the idea of a specific school focus for every school, 60% accept that there is a need for public evaluation of schools, and 80% are willing to practice interior self-evaluation of their school focus (Lehmpfuhl and Rolff 1996, p. 11).

A new legitimation of the school as an institution is seen as being necessary because more and more students do not accept the idea that learning in schools is a prerequisite for a successful life. Too many students have observed that a good education does not guarantee a good career or a high standard of living. There are too many academics, parents, relatives, and friends who are unemployed, regardless of their education. Students also notice that many teachers are unsure about their instructional tasks, about the values they ought to transmit to the children. In particular, students in vocational schools note the gap between school requirements and the knowledge and skills they will need when they face the world of work in businesses, industrial plants, or laboratories.

The curriculum *is* changing, however slow the process may seem. Abstract content knowledge is no longer sufficient, because students realize that such knowledge does not, in itself, prevent wars, clean up environmental pollution, or protect human rights. Students want practical, authentic knowledge. And this desire, coupled with workplace realities and the explosion of information, affects how society defines the role of the teacher — and how teachers define their roles for themselves.

Whereas the training of elementary and Hauptschule teachers includes the study of pedagogy, psychology, and didactics, all other teachers — Gymnasium, Gesamtschule, university, and so on — are trained primarily in the specific subjects that they will teach. Thus most secondary level teachers are knowledgeable in their subjects but not necessarily in pedagogy. A change from this content orientation to a more student-oriented instructional approach is seen as essential, because the content-oriented, teacher-driven model of instruction is no longer well-accepted by students. The traditional position of the teacher as a knowledge expert has been shaken. Consequently, recent studies of the profession of teaching have led to a broad advocacy for more training for potential secondary teachers in pedagogy and educational psychology.

Finally, because the school has lost some of its reputation as a state institution and the traditional delivery of knowledge is not accepted as the primary goal that it once was, schools are beginning to reconsider teaching and curriculum. Teachers, administrators, and other education authorities have begun the serious task of asking students about *their* needs and desires. Teachers, both newcomers and veterans, have turned to more student-centered teaching approaches. And the school curriculum — both broadly and in specific subjects — is more often determined by the students than by a fixed syllabus handed down by the Ministry of Education. In classrooms across Germany, traditional, formal, teacher-led lessons are being supplemented by projects; and the school is opening to real life.

These actions represent a fundamental change in the direction of German schools. And this constitutes promise for the future.

No fundamental change can be realized in a short time. The process for German schools — in particular, secondary schools — has just begun. There is still doubt about whether the school as a traditional and static institution *can* actually change. But today's politicians, school administrators, scholars, teachers, and parents are accepting the need for basic change. And so it is likely that German schools in the future will look quite different from those that exist today.

REFERENCES

Berg, H.C., and Steffens, U. *Schulqualität und Schulvielfalt*. Wiesbaden, 1991.

Bildungskommission NRW. *Zukunft der Bildung, Schule der Zukunft*. Neuwied: Luchterhand Verlag, 1995.

Deutscher Ausschuß für das Erziehungs- und Bildungswesen. *Rahmenplan zur Umgestaltung und Vereinbeitlichung des Allgemeinbildenden Öffentlichen Schulwesens*. Stuttgart: Ernst Klett Verlag, 1959.

Deutscher Bildungsrat. *Strukturplan für das Bildungswesen*. Stuttgart: Ernst Klett Verlag, 1970.

"Effective Schools: A Review." *Elementary School Journal* 4 (1983): 426-52.

Fend, Helmut. *Gesamtschule im Vergleich: Bilanz der Ergebnisse des Gesamtschulversuchs*. Weinheim: Beltz Verlag, 1982.

Hage, K.; Bischoff, H.; Dichanz, H.; et al. *Das Methodenrepertoire von Lehrern*. Opladen: Leske and Budrich, 1985.

Liket, Theo M.E. *Freiheit und Verantwortung: Das Niederländische Modell des Bildungswesens*. Gutersloh: Verlag Bertelsmann-Stiftung, 1993.

Lehmpfuhl, Uwe, and Rolff, Hans-Günter. "Leitbild Statt Leiden." *Neue Deutsche Schule* 6 (1996): 10-13.

Rolff, Hans-Gunter; Bauer, Karl-Oswald; Klemm, Klaus; and Pfeiffer, Hermann. *Jahrbuch der Schulentwicklung Bd. 6*. Weinheim/München: Juventa Verlag, 1990.

Tillmann, Klaus-Jürgen. "Staatlicher Zusammenbruch und Schulischer Wandel. Schultheoretische Reflexionen zum Deutsch-Deutschen Einigungsprozess." In *Zietschrift für Pädagogik* 30 (1993): 29-36.

Tillmann, Klaus-Jürgen. "Von der Kontinuität, die nicht auffällt: Das Schulsystem vom Übergang von der DDR zur BRD." In *Zeitschrift für Pädagogik* 32 (1994): 264-66.

Weishaupt, Horst, and Zedler, Peter. "Aspekte der aktuellen Schulentwicklung in den neuen Ländern." In *Jahrbuch der Schulentwicklung Bd. 8*. Weinheim/München: Juventa Verlag, 1994.

Zahorik, J., and Dichanz, H. "Teaching for Understanding in German Elementary Schools." *Educational Leadership* 51 (1994): 75-77.

ABOUT THE AUTHORS

Dr. Horst Dichanz is a professor of education in "Erziehungs-, Sozial-, und Geisteswissenschaften" (education, social sciences, and humanities) at FernUniversität, a Gesamthochschule in Hagen, Germany.

Dr. John A. Zahorik is a professor in the Department of Curriculum and Instruction, School of Education, at the University of Wisconsin-Milwaukee.